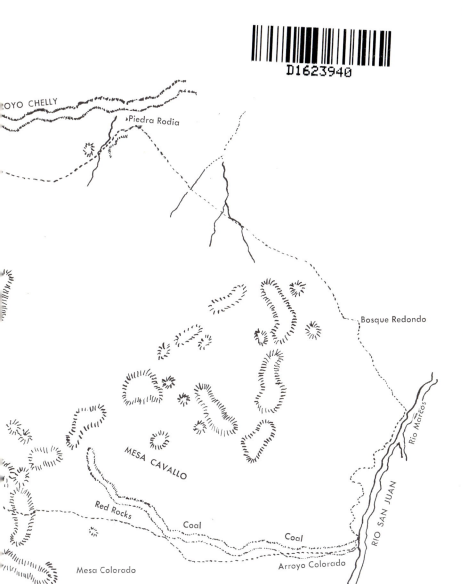

OYO CHELLY

Piedra Rodia

Bosque Redondo

Rio Marcos

MESA CAVALLO

RIO SAN JUAN

Red Rocks

Coal

Coal

Mesa Colorado

Arroyo Colorado

D1623940

CONNECTICUT COLLEGE FOR WOMEN
· 1911 ·
· NEW LONDON ·

&~ *The Gift of*

THE FIFTIETH ANNIVERSARY
FUND

CONNECTICUT COLLEGE
LIBRARY

THE NAVAJO
RECONNAISSANCE

GREAT WEST AND INDIAN SERIES XXV
WESTERN SURVEY SERIES III

AN EDITION OF 600 COPIES ONLY

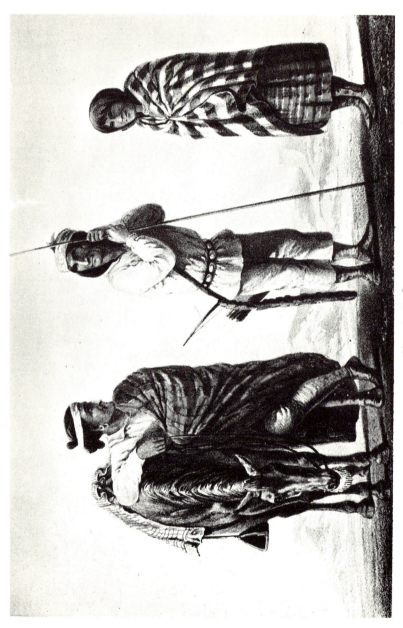

Navajo Indians

—Courtesy Southwest Museum.

THE NAVAJO RECONNAISSANCE

A Military Exploration of the Navajo Country in 1859

by
CAPTAIN J. G. WALKER
and
MAJOR O. L. SHEPHERD

with foreword, annotations and index
by L. R. BAILEY

WESTERNLORE PRESS . . . 1964 . . . LOS ANGELES 41

917.91
W152

COPYRIGHT 1964 BY

WESTERNLORE PRESS

Library of Congress Catalog No. 64-18547

PRINTED IN THE UNITED STATES OF AMERICA BY WESTERNLORE PRESS

CONTENTS

vii

245933

ILLUSTRATIONS

FOREWORD

WITHIN ninety days of declaration of war against Mexico by the United States, General Stephen W. Kearny was in Santa Fe. In an August 1846 proclamation, Kearny promised and assured the conquered Mexican populace of the Southwest that the Anglo-American military would, from that time forward, protect them from the marauding bands of Indians that had plagued them for a century. Kearny, however, quickly discovered that this pledge amounted to a rather large order. The declaration had scarcely circulated before the Navajos, occupying the red-rock country of northwest New Mexico and northeast Arizona, staged a vicious series of raids against their hereditary enemies—the Mexicans and Pueblo Indians.

Lieutenant Colonel Alexander Doniphan, following orders from General Kearny, conducted the first Anglo-American expedition against the Navajos. With 350 soldiers of the First Missouri Volunteers, he temporarily sidetracked his military objective in the Mexican War to march against the bothersome tribe; and at Ojo del Oso (Bear Springs), on the north slopes of the Zuñi Mountains, fifteen miles east of present-day Gallup, New Mexico, Doniphan concluded the first treaty with the Navajo Indians. This peace treaty, however, proved to be a mere scrap of paper; and between its signing (on November 22, 1946) and the summer of 1849, several other Anglo-American punitive editions were launched against the tribe—but in vain. Navajo depredations still continued at an alarming rate.

In late summer 1849, Brevet Lt. Col. John M. Washington, military commander of New Mexico, personally led another expedition against the tribe. His command consisted of 175 seasoned American troopers, augmented by a contingent of New Mexican volunteers. They entered the Navajo country by way of Chaco Cañon, and proceeded to the western mouth of Cañon de Chelly, near Chinle, after killing a prominent Navajo headman, Narbona, near Two Grey Hills. On a knoll, a hundred yards north of present-day Thunderbird Ranch, Washington held council with chiefs Zarcillas Largas, Chapiton, and Mariano Martinez. These Navajos solemnly agreed that their people would retire from raiding the New Mexican settlements—and another peace treaty was signed. Before Colonel Washington had returned to the Rio Grande, however, Navajo raiding parties struck.

Punitive expeditions and peace treaties apparently had little effect on the accepted Navajo way of life. The tribe was split in numerous clans and bands having little if any influence over one another; and contrary to Anglo-American beliefs at that time, Navajo headmen possessed only limited control. In 1850, Hugh Smith, New Mexico's congressman, complained that the Navajos had no respect whatever for the authority of the United States Government. He cited reports from the office of the United States Marshal that, between October 1, 1846, and October 1, 1850, the Navajos and their Apache cousins had stolen from New Mexican settlements, 12,887 mules, 7,000 horses, 31,581 cattle and 453,293 sheep.

Although no doubt exaggerated, these reports of depredations were disturbing to civil and military authorities, who were bound to protect New Mexico, as well as the northern states of Mexico from the aggressions of Indian tribes. In Washington, Secretary of War C. M. Conrad sought means to strengthen frontier defenses; and by 1851 drastic plans had been drawn up for the reorganization of the Army in the West. The first step in that direction was the choosing of a competent officer as commander-in-chief of troops in New Mexico. A soldier of considerable frontier experience was selected for the task—Colonel Edwin Vose Sumner.

Sumner's first steps in carrying out the orders of the War Department was to withdraw those garrisons lying inactive in New Mexican communities and concentrate them closer to frontier points. The new commander was in the territory but one month before he tackled the Navajo problem. In mid-August 1851, he marched into Navajo country with four companies of mounted troops, one company of artillery, and two of infantry. Sumner, like his predecessors, marched directly to that reputed Navajo stronghold—Cañon de Chelly—hoping to impress the recalcitrant tribesmen with an overwhelming display of strength. However, Sumner had penetrated the chasm's depths only a short distance before he grew fearful of the unknown terrain, and retraced his steps. At Cañon Bonito, six miles north of present-day Window Rock, Arizona, the colonel determined to build a post of sufficient strength which would quell the Navajos—and he named it appropriately Fort Defiance.

Fort Defiance rose on the site of an old Navajo rendezvous near the spot where Bonito Creek joined Black Creek; and garrisoned it with five companies. The construction of this post was no small undertaking, but a new determination had entered the American military, and soon a quadrangle of adobe, stone and log barracks, and officers' quarters encompassed the parade ground.

With this dagger pointed at their very heart, the Navajos became considerably less ebullient. Depredations became less, and civil and military authorities deemed it time to appoint someone to represent the interest of the tribe. Although in years past there were other men chosen as Navajo agents, Henry Linn Dodge would be the first agent to actually live and mingle with his charges.

Henry Linn Dodge, son of Senator Henry Dodge of Wisconsin, and brother to Augustus Ceasar Dodge, Senator from Missouri, was a seasoned soldier and frontiersman. He had served with the Army in its Rocky Mountain explorations and Santa Fe trail escorts, and was a veteran of Colonel Washington's 1849 expedition into Navajo country. Knowing the military, and with full sympathy and understanding of the Navajos, Dodge was by far the best selection possible as an agent to deal with this people. With great tact and courage he established his agency near the eastern approach to Washington Pass, above Sheep Springs. There he erected his agency headquarters, and brought to it George Carter, an ex-soldier and blacksmith, to teach his charges iron-smithing. Dodge brought also Juan Anea, one of the finest of Mexican silversmiths. With fearlessness and devotion to duty unparalleled among United States Indian agents at that time, Dodge for three years kept the Navajos at peace, and out of the vindictive clutches of the military and civil leaders of New Mexico. Unfortunately for the people he so bravely and conscientiously served, and for the history of Anglo-American Indian relations, Dodge was kidnaped and murdered by Coyotero Apaches in mid-November 1856.

After the death of Dodge, Navajos were represented either by agents who had no stomach for the rough and hazardous life demanded in that red-rock country, or by no agent at all. This job was a political plum with few takers, and those who did take it perferred to handle Navajo affairs from behind the barricades at Fort Defiance, or from the even safer havens of Santa Fe or Albuquerque. Added to the lack of administrative zeal of the Indian Department were the clamors now being voiced by New Mexican politicians and livestock owners who sought to enrich themselves at the Indian's expense. Demands were simple—immediate war, appropriation of Navajo herds and flocks, or the complete removal of the tribe to some remote reservation and the division of Navajo lands among white settlers of the Southwest. Added to this, was the fact that the military itched for the opening of hostilities.

Plagued by land-hungry New Mexican sheepmen and slave-raiders from frontier towns, the Navajos walked into the virtual trap set for them. During the early spring of 1858, Navajos launched a number of reprisal raids. The real war, however, broke out at Fort Defiance. On July 12, 1858, a Negro servant belonging to the commandant, Major W. T. H. Brooks was mortally wounded by a Navajo. A full explanation of the incident and surrender of the murderer was immediately demanded by Brooks. Navajo headmen instead, suggested that blood-money be paid—for it was not within their power to turn over the culprit.

To Major Brooks this was not a satisfactory answer; and he gave the tribe twenty days in which to produce the killer, or face a war to the finish. To satisfy the irate major, the Navajos brought in the corpse of a Mexican slave and tried to pass it off as that of the murderer—a further insult and provocation for war! Military movements against the tribesmen came in rapid succession. The campaign was entrusted to Colonel Dixon S. Miles, who left Fort Defiance on September 9 with 310 men of the Third Infantry and Mounted Rifles, bound for Cañon de Chelly. His march was a long and fruitless one, for the Navajos merely vanished into the recesses of their red-rock country. Another sortie was attempted, this time eastward over the Chuska Mountains at Tohatchi, thence northward to Sanastee. Doubling back, Miles crossed through Washington Pass and proceeded to Fort Defiance—and this mission also fell far short of expectation. In October, Miles and Major Backus, the first commander of Fort Defiance, led forth columns in a combined operation against the Navajos. The two commands, guided by Ute and New Mexican auxiliaries, skirted both sides of the Tunicha-Chuska Mountains, reaching a point at the northern extremities of the Tunichas, then striking westward to Cañon de Chelly. With the conclusion of this campaign and the approach of the "holiday season," the enthusiasm of the military at Fort Defiance waned. An armistice of thirty-days duration was signed by the military and Navajo headmen; and this was followed by an official treaty conference on Christmas Day 1858.

Under the terms of this peace treaty, the Navajos agreed to restore or pay for all property taken from New Mexican settlements during the fall of 1858. The entire tribe would in the future be responsible for depredations committed by any of its members. All Pueblo and New Mexican captives would be surrendered; and tribal boundaries were set on a line running north from a point fourteen miles west of Zuñi Pueblo, passing through Bear Springs and continuing northward to the juncture of the Chaco and San Juan Rivers. In short, the Navajos lost all prime grazing and agricultural lands lying to the east of the Chuska-Tunicha Mountains.

For four months following the conclusion of the Treaty of 1858, the Navajos attempted to satisfy its demands. Beginning in January, tribal headmen sent into Fort Defiance small lots of livestock in an effort to repay New Mexicans for losses amounting to almost 6,000 animals, valued at more than $14,000. Several captives, stolen at early ages from Rio Grande settlements, were also brought in. These individuals, however, were now Indian in every sense of the word; and when given the choice of returning to their Mexican families or remaining with the Indians, they chose the latter. They had lived as Indians so long that they had lost the Spanish tongue, and considered the vermilion mesas and cañons of Navajoland their true homes. When one captive was offered his freedom, he replied, "the Navajos were his brothers and his friends, and with them he desired to live."

This evidence of good faith on the part of the headmen induced the Office of Indian Affairs to dispatch to Fort Defiance, the annuity goods which had been withheld from the tribe during the past conflict. And in early April "a liberal allowance" of annuities were issued to assembled tribesmen at Fort Defiance; and in return a few more horses were accepted by the military as further evidence that the Navajos were at least attempting to comply with the terms of the 1858 Treaty.

No matter how well intending Navajo headmen were, they could never guarantee the conduct of the greater portion of their tribe. During the spring months of 1859 there were once again reports of raids and plunderings.

On May 13 prominent rancher, Henry Connelly, informed Superintendent of Indian Affairs James L. Collins, that 2,000 sheep belonging to Felipe Chavez had been driven off; and that two herders employed by the Padillas lay dead. The slaying of the two *pastores* brought threats of open reprisals by New Mexicans. There were bitter complaints voiced against the military, when demands for the murderers of these men were not pressed—as had been done in the case of Major Brooks' Negro servant.

Superintendent of Indian Affairs James Collins was convinced that Navajo leaders had little or no influence; and on May 29 he informed Commissioner of Indian Affairs Greenwood, that "the influential men seem entirely unable to control the dishonest portion of the tribe, and in many cases it is believed . . . they connive at the robberies committed by their people." The raids against New Mexican flocks substantiated the superintendent's belief that the armistice and treaty had been too hasty; and he suggested more stringent measures be taken against the tribe:

> It is true that since the conclusion of peace the conduct of the chiefs had led me to hope that the tribe would profit by the lesson they had received. But their chastisement must be more severe, they must be well punished and thoroughly humbled before we can expect better conduct from them.

Although Collins acknowledged that recent reports of Navajo depredations might have been exaggerated by New Mexicans, hoping for greater indemnity and a justifiable cause for launching reprisals; still he believed that a show of force was necessary to force tribal compliance with treaty terms.

By mid-May Commander of the Department of New Mexico, Colonel Benjamin E. L. Bonneville, had taken steps to force the Indians into line. An expedition was planned and organized under the command of Major John S. Simonson, of the Mounted Rifles. The orders carried by this illustrious officer and veteran of the Mexican War, stipulated a movement through Navajoland as a demonstration of the might of the United States military—without actually bringing on a full-scale Indian war. A series of exploratory expeditions were projected to seek out grazing localities, planting grounds, and points of Navajo habitation. All this vital information would be reported in detail, and the country mapped thoroughly for future reference in event of war with the tribe.

On June 12, Simonson assumed command of the expedition numbering 700 men, which would march in two columns for Fort Defiance. The portion of the command assembling at Las Lunas, would march by way of Laguna and Cubero on June 17. The other column, commanded personally by the major, would take the road from Abiquiu to Cañon Bonito via Ojo Caliente, crossing the Tunicha Mountains, twenty-five miles northwest of Washington Pass.

Reaching Fort Defiance about the first of July, Major Simonson immediately requested Navajo leaders to assemble for a series of "talks," before Army scouting parties were sent out. Between July 5 to 14, Simonson held three councils. The first two meetings effected little owing to poor attendance of the headmen, who were afraid to approach too near the post. To dispel Navajo suspicions, the last meeting (July 14), was held in a wooded area about a mile from Fort Defiance; and was attended by Herrero, Zarcillas Largas, and a number of other prominent chiefs. At this council, "an article of agreement" was put forward for the signature of the headmen. This document was intended—if signed by the Navajos—to bind them to restoration of all property (or its equivalent) stolen since the conclusion of peace, as well as that stolen by them since August 15, 1858. However, Herrero and Zarcillas Largas had seen enough of these pieces of paper and knew how much reliance Anglos put upon them. They persuaded the other headmen not to sign the "agreement." But the chiefs verbally pledged to repay all they had stolen.

On the day of the last council with Navajo headmen, Major Simonson issued Orders No. 8, authorizing the organization of two commands to explore the western portion of Navajoland. Four days later the reconnaissances were ready to undertake the task assigned them. The column commanded by Captain John George Walker, a native of Missouri, and veteran of the Mexican War, consisted of companies C, G, Third Infantry; and company K, and detachment from E, Mounted Rifles.

Leaving its assembling point at Camp La Joya near Fort Defiance, Walker's command headed northward to the eastern mouth of Cañon de Chelly; and on the morning of July 20, entered the chasm "half a mile below the mouth" of present-day Wheatfield Creek—one of three streams forming the eastern portion of the Rio Chelly. For two days Walker and his troops moved down the collosal cañon without molesting Indian crops. Past Monument Cañon, and "the lofty and spire-like pillar" of Spider Rock, Walker's command moved, and on to the famous White House Ruin, near the juncture of Cañon del Muerto and Cañon de Chelly, close to present day Chinle, Arizona.

On July 22, Walker's reconnaissance moved up the Chinle Wash, passing a succession of Navajo fields, probably near Many Farms; and on the 23rd reached present-day Round Rock, located eighteen miles north of Chinle. For the next five days the command moved northeastward, and finally struck the Rio San Juan, near the famous "Four Corners" area. From there, Walker skirted the eastern flanks of the Carrizo Mountains, crossed Redrock Valley, and passed between the Lukachukai and Tunicha mountains. Marching down the western slopes of the Tunichas, Walker and his tired troops reached Camp La Joya by August 1.

The second expedition, which left at the same time that Walker's did, was commanded by Captain Oliver Lathrop Shepherd, of New York, also a veteran of the Mexican War. The command consisted of companies B, K, and a portion of G, Third Infantry, as well as company H, and part of G, Mounted Rifles. This column marched westward from Fort Defiance toward the Moqui (Hopi) villages. Although not as detailed as Walker's report, that of Shepherd's revealed interesting facts pertaining to many localities along the famous "Moqui Road," between Fort Defiance and the Little Colorado, as well as to the country lying southward, near Wide Ruins. During the course of this exploration (which covered nearly 205 miles), Shepherd's command passed over what is perhaps the poorest section of the Navajo country, and consequently observed few Indians, fields and flocks. However, they did find evidence of grazing grounds, where Navajos had moved their sheep and horses to lower elevations to protect them from the killing blasts of winter; as well as observing "a thousand acres or so" of corn fields planted by Hopis.

Almost a month after the conclusion of the first two reconnaissances, Major Simonson again authorized two more explorations, and entrusted them to the commanders of the previous ones. On September 5, Lieutenant J. G. Walker again marched from Fort Defiance, with company K, and portions of E, Mounted Rifles; and companies C and E, Third Infantry—this time heading for Mesa de la Vaca or Black Mesa, and the country to the north.

Crossing the central portion of Black Mesa, Walker proceeded northwestward to present-day Klethlana Valley, which separates the rugged northern escarpment of Black Mesa from the extremely dissected country south of Navajo Mountain—which he called Sierra Panoche. Moving through Klethlana Valley to Marsh Pass, Walker struck southward, again toward Cañon de Chelly; and on September 18 passed along that cañon's southern rim, and on the next day marched for Ewell's Hay Camp, ten miles north of Fort Defiance.

It was near Cañon de Chelly, that Walker learned of outside influences at work attempting to turn the Navajos against the United States Government. He had been informed that Mormons from Utah were working among the tribesmen. This religious sect which had fled persecution in Illinois and Missouri to found their Zion in the Great Basin, was now under attack by the United States Army. Consequently missionaries, who in the past had preached salvation, were now acting as spies, attempting to stir western tribes against the "Gentiles." Walker had been told that Mormons were seeking to unite all tribes between the Colorado and the Rio Grande, "to resist encroachment of the people and government of the United States, the natural enemies of the whole Indian race." The Mormons, according to Walker, had deputized Paiutes to visit the Navajos and invite them to a council at Navajo Mountain, to be held in mid-October—at which guns, powder, and other articles of trade would be passed out to assembled tribesmen. And Walker perceptively warned in his report, that "should a war break out between our troops and the tribes . . . it will have been brought about to no inconsiderable degree by Mormon influence and intrigue."

The same time that Lieutenant John G. Walker was marching toward Navajo Mountain, Captain Oliver L. Shepherd, with almost the same command he had during the survey of country south of Hopi, was being detailed to make a thorough examination of the foremost zone of conflict between the Navajos and New Mexicans—Mount San Mateo and the Zuñi Mountains. On September 5 Shepherd and his troops left Fort Defiance, crossed the fertile Chuska Valley, and skirted the northern slopes of the Zuñi Mountains, passing within a short distance of Ojo del Oso (Bear Springs). From that traditional Navajo rendezvous, the command headed for the north and west slopes of Mount San Mateo—later to be renamed Mount Taylor.

To Shepherd, this portion of the Navajo country lying contiguous to the New Mexican communities of Cebolleta and Cubero, as well as the pueblos of Laguna and Acoma, seemed alive with Navajo signs; and he biasly wrote in his official report: "The whole route thus far had the most numerous and heavily beaten trails, I have ever seen in the Navajo country, and it is evidently the great thoroughfare for all thefts and robberies."

Leaving the frontier settlements of Cebolleta and Cubero, Shepherd on September 14, passed the extensive field of lava lying southwest of Mount Taylor; and three days later arrived at the Saline Lake, south of Zuñi Pueblo. Long a neutral ground for not only Navajos, but Puebloans, and Apaches, this salina impressed Shepherd. There he found well-beaten trails: some leading west toward the Little Colorado River; others eastward to the pueblos and New Mexican settlements—all made by peoples forgetting their grievances momentarily to gather the precious salt. The military reconnaissance delayed its march nearly a whole day while its commander examined and recorded pertinent observations about this natural feature, before resuming the route to Zuñi, and Fort Defiance beyond.

Thus ended the most complete reconnaissance of Navajoland made since the inception of Anglo-American occupation of New Mexico. From data gathered during the course of these four explorations, Major John S. Simonson was convinced that the majority of Navajos desired peace; and from the vast numbers of sheep and horses observed, the tribesmen could comply with the terms of the December treaty. Consequently on September 25, Major Simonson, Lieutenant Walker and Indian Agent Silas F. Kendrick, informed headmen that the tribe would be given thirty days in which to indemnify New Mexican livestock losses.

During the weeks that followed, events would occur at Fort Defiance which would change the picture of Anglo-Navajo relations and set the stage for full-scale hostilities. Throughout October Navajos turned over small quantities of livestock to the military—but not without complaint. The Indians bitterly related that their people had been killed, their property stolen—and they had not been offered compensation for any part of *their* losses. Regardless of what the tribesmen had sustained, they were still obligated to pay the claims—half of which, they alleged, were fictitious. Added to the Navajo change of tune, was a change in command at that isolated frontier post. Because of failing health, the sympathetic, amiable, Major John S. Simonson had asked for, and been granted a transfer of duty. In his place, Captain Oliver Lathrop Shepherd, an officer devoid of understanding for the Indians and seeking only personal glory and promotion, had been chosen commandant of the Navajo Command.

By October 25—the expiration of the period allowed the Navajos for indemnification of stolen stock—only 19 horses, and 130 sheep had been delivered to Fort Defiance. According to calculations by the military and the Office of Indian Affairs, the value of these animals amounted to only one-tenth of the outstanding claim—which exceeded $14,000. Thus disappointed in his hopes that the Navajos would still comply with treaty stipulations, Agent Kendrick on October 25, officially laid his charges in the hands of the new military commander, Captain O. L. Shepherd:

> Having used every means within my power as agent for the Navajo Indians to obtain from them a compliance with the stipulations . . ., and these means having entirely failed to induce such compliance. It now becomes my duty under my instructions from the Superintendent of Indian Affairs . . . to bring officially to their knowledge the delinquency of the tribe, and to apply to you as the commanding officer . . . at this post to enforce the provisions of that engagement or treaty.

In early November an escort was furnished Agent Kendrick to conduct the stock which the Indians had turned over safely to Albuquerque, there to be either sold or delivered to persons having suffered at the hands of the Indians. During this trip an incident occurred, which together with others, greatly precipitated matters.

The first night after leaving Fort Defiance, Navajos stampeded all but eighteen horses which the agent had charge of. The following morning an Indian on horseback, carrying two U.S. rifles, was discovered lurking about camp. With promises of protection, Kendrick lured the buck into camp. When questioned about the guns, the Navajo stated that he had found the weapons, but would cheerfully give them up for "some trivial reward." The officer in charge of the escort, Lieutenant Walker, induced the Indian to take a letter to Fort Defiance, informing Major Shepherd of the loss of the horses. The Indian faithfully performed the mission—though somewhat tardily. In recompense for his trouble, Major Shepherd ordered a severe flogging to be administered to the Indian's bare back. As the Navajo belonged to the band of Ganado Mucho, one of the most faithful friends of the Anglos, this wanton beating greatly shook the confidence which this band had for United States authority.

Agent Kendrick returned to Cañon Bonito on December 18. Shortly thereafter several leading Navajos came to him begging that the tribe be permitted until January 1 to satisfy the indemnification demands. But Kendrick replied that he no longer had control in the matter; and that the tribesmen would have to apply directly to the post commander. From that time until mid-January, few Indians ventured into Fort Defiance. The atmosphere of Anglo-Navajo relations at that isolated military post carried the current of impending storm.

At sundown on January 15, a Navajo headman, Juan-ico, requested a conference with the agent on the hill overlooking the fort. Kendrick suspecting treachery, requested the Indian to come into the post. When the latter refused, an interpreter was sent out to learn the object of the visit. The Indian revealed that small parties of Navajos had been passing his ranchería all day, going in the direction of the grazing camp, seven miles from the post—as if intending to attack the military herd. This information was immediately communicated to Major Shepherd, who dispatched a detachment of thirty men to strengthen the guard at that point. The next morning another chief, Agua Chiquito, came into Fort Defiance and informed Kendrick that Herrero, the "Head Chief" of the tribe, was the instigator of the proposed attack.

The information which the two Indians relayed was correct. Just after sunrise on the morning of January 17, the cattle herd was attack by 200-300 Navajos. The raid would have succeeded had it not been for the reinforcement of the guard. The warriors were beaten off by the vigilant soldiers, with only a few oxen lost. However, on their retreat, the Indians attacked a wood detail of four soldiers and killed three. At noon the same day still another detachment from Fort Defiance, which was sawing lumber three miles distant, was surprised. Again the Anglo soldiers paid with the blood of another man killed, and one wounded. The Navajos tried desperately to cut off the much-needed supplies, now en route to the virtually desieged troops at Cañon Bonito. The quartermaster train sent out from Albuquerque was constantly harassed by the Indians, as it snaked its way deeper into Navajoland; and would probably have been lost altogether had it not been for the presences of an escort of forty-two men under the command of Lieutenant William Dickinson.

With the eruption of war with the Navajos came a breach between the Indian Department and the military. The incident which severed all connections between the two, occurred on January 20. Early that morning the friendly chief, Agua Chiquito made his appearance on the brow of the hill overlooking the fort, and was invited into the post by Major Shepherd and the Indian Agent—on the assurance that he would not be hurt. This headman appeared anxious to talk only to Kendrick. When the latter proceeded to confer with the Indian through an interpreter, the officer abruptly interrupted the conference, and informed the agent that he was in command, and that the representative of the Indian Department would hereafter not be allowed to converse with any Navajo without prior permission. Shepherd then endeavored to "talk" with Chiquito. When the Indian did not show an interest in what the commander was saying, Shepherd became enraged, and ordered him to leave the post. As the Indian turned to go, the major instructed the sentinels to fire on him. Agua Chiquito, however, quickly darted out of the post and made his way to safety.

Shepherd's actions had alienated the last vestige of Navajo goodwill. In his final report (dated February 25, 1860), Agent Kendrick wrote:

"Up to this occurrence Agua Chiquito, Ganado Mucho, Juanico and several other influential members of the tribe, had given every evidence of their sincere desire to bring their people to an amicable adjustment of the difficulties and had rendered many valuable services to me and also to the military . . . . There was every reason to believe in and rely upon their good faith, and they were extremely anxious to second and advance the views and purposes of the Government to the best of their ability. But since this treatment of Agua Chiquito, not one of these Indians has returned to . . . the Fort or to seek any communication with me or with any other white man. Evidently their good confidence in the good faith of the Americans is entirely destroyed, and if they have not become active combatants themselves, they cannot be expected again to cooperate with us."

Following the alienation of Agua Chiquito, Major Shepherd wrote to the agent, again warning him not to confer with the Indians; and that if the instructions were violated, he would be ordered from the post. Since his arrival in Navajoland in early September, Kendrick had attempted not to tread upon military toes. When councils were held, he journeyed to them without escort. He accepted whatever quarters were provided for his agency; and had always informed the post commander of any actions taken by the Indian Department. Silas Kendrick felt that Shepherd's actions and subsequent letter was a direct affront to himself and a hindrance to the endeavors of the Office of Indian Affairs—as well as a treacherous act which put the army little above the savages they were now fighting. Agent Kendrick could not leave the major's note unanswered. On January 20, he accordingly responded in writing:

> SIR: I have just received your note of today informing me that war now existed with the Navajo Indians, and that I am prohibited from holding within this garrison, any intercourse with this tribe, and that the first violation of this order, I must be prepared to leave the post.
>
> It seems that a change has taken place in your mind since this morning. I asked you to let me talk to the Indians [in] your presence and you refused. I give you notice now, as I told you today, that I will talk to them when I please outside of the post.
>
> If your note is intended as a threat I pass it by unnoticed as one would the passing fly that should perchance light upon his head. I will discharge my duty as agent regardless of consequences.
>
> I will now notify you that your conduct in reference to the Indians—the Navajos that you invited into the Post this morning and other circumstances shall bring you officially before the proper tribunal for adjustment.

As war now existed with the Navajos, Agent Kendrick saw little use in remaining at Fort Defiance. On January 23, he requested permission of Superintendent Collins to return to Santa Fe, which was granted on February 5.

New Mexico was now in the grips of another full-scale Indian war. News of Navajo depredations poured in daily. The commander of the military department, Colonel Thomas T. Fauntleroy (who had replaced Col. B. L. E. Bonneville), remained inactive. The forces stationed throughout the territory had never been so strong. Twenty-two companies of infantry and mounted troops were at the immediate disposal of the commander—if and when he chose to move. Despite the availability of

1800 fully equipped soldiers, Fauntleroy hesitated, and requested authority to call upon the governor for an additional 1,000 volunteers, as well as recruitment of 400 Utes. In the meantime, Fauntleroy informed the commander of Fort Defiance that no expedition would be launched against the Navajos. However, the troops at that post must, at all costs, keep communications open to Albuquerque.

Such hesitancy on the part of the army, together with increasing livestock losses, created considerable agitation from the territory's general population. Outbreaks of public opinion protested the inadequate protection along the frontier. By spring this feeling was becoming so intense it was venting itself in the organization of irregular companies to invade Navajoland. The Territorial Assembly, influenced by popular demand, passed a bill authorizing the organization and conduct of an independent campaign. Governor Abraham Rencher authorized the raising of two companies of militia, each 100 men strong, and armed them. The Utes, who had always sided with the New Mexicans against the Navajos, were influenced to raid their southern neighbors. At Abiquiu, Ute Agent Albert W. Pheiffer, openly encouraged his charges to conduct attacks; and his agency was used as a rendezvous for combined expeditions made up of New Mexicans, Utes and even Apaches.

In the meantime, Navajo raids in the vicinity of Fort Defiance became better organized, and more frequent. On February 8, the cattle guard, consisting of three commissioned officers and forty-one privates, was attacked at Ewell's Hay Camp by an estimated 500 Navajos, who were finally repulsed after a two-hour battle. The lines of communication with Albuquerque—the supply depot for the garrison—were constantly cut by the marauders. It was with great difficulty that the four companies constituting the garrison, were able to keep their livestock intact, as well as provide strong escorts for the quartermaster trains supplying the fort.

Regardless of increased pressure upon the already strained troops at Fort Defiance, orders were dispatched from department headquarters, directing Company G, Third Infantry, to proceed on April 21 to Ojo del Oso, where a new post (Fort Fauntleroy) was being constructed as another barrier to Navajo incursions. The Indians, witnessing the weakened state of Fort Defiance, launched an attack directly at the post nine days later.

About four o'clock on the morning of April 30, 1860, an estimated 1,000 Indians closed in upon Fort Defiance. Because of the terrain surrounding this fort, Navajos were able to approach undetected from three sides. With war-whoops and yells, the warriors closed in. Through the corrals they poured, driving in the sentinels. The three companies comprising the garrison instantly turned out and took positions of defense. A part of Company C, Third Infantry, attempted to get into the kitchen gardens on the west side of the post but were driven back to the sheltering walls of the bake-house and laundress quarters by the heavy fire of Navajos, screened behind the fences and wood piles.

For awhile it looked as if the Navajos would take Fort Defiance. Warriors seemed to be everywhere. Indians penetrated the sutler's quarters and were rifling the goods stored in the back rooms. They were behind, and in the post's outhouses. Frantically the troops endeavored to stem the tide which threatened to engulf them. Lieutenant A. W. Whipple, with E Company, was detailed to clear and secure the magazine, corrals and stables containing the officers' mounts and work teams. On the east side of the post, Company B, under Lieutenant William Dickinson, took up a position between the fort and the abrupt hill rising behind.

By dawn the Navajo attack was spent, and the Indians were withdrawing up the hillsides, leaving their dead behind. Lieutenant Hildt was ordered to take Company C, and pursue the retreating savages. This order, however, was countermanded when the advancing troops, mistaken for Indians, were fired upon by soldiers in the post below. When light enough for the troops to distinguish one another, Company C was again deployed, along with B Company, to clear the mesa tops to the east and north. The Navajos, as usual, faded away before the advancing soldiers, and the latter returned with nothing to show for their labors.

This brazen attack upon Fort Defiance acted as a stimulus for army operations. On May 4, the Adjutant General of the Army ordered that the post be not abandoned "for the time being;" and Secretary of War, J. B. Floyd issued the following declaration:

Active operations will be instituted against the Navajos as soon as the necessary preparations can be made. A winter campaign *with infantry,* if inaugurated with secrecy and prosecuted with vigor, will prove the shortest and most effectual plan of operations.

For the next two months the army geared itself for a full-scale campaign, the likes of which the Territory of New Mexico had never before witnessed.

PUBLISHER'S NOTE: We wish to acknowledge the Army and Navy Branch of the National Archives, Washington, D.C., for their kind help in securing the military reports and documents comprising this volume. The style and phraseology of the original reports have been followed. Only in cases of obvious misspellings, has the copy been corrected.

Fort Defiance, 1855

—*Schoolcraft.*

INTRODUCTORY LETTER

Fort Defiance, N. M.
August 8, 1859

SIR:

I have the honor herewith to forward reports of Bvt. Major Shepherd and Captain Walker, Commanders of Columns of Exploration in the Navajo country. These reports are very interesting, the explorations having been made through a portion of the country heretofore unexamined by our troops. The officers and men deserve much credit for the manner in which this duty has been executed during a very inclement season.

Since my last report the conduct of the Indians had been pacific. Herrero Miles[1] and Zarcillas Largas,[2] notwithstanding their refusal to sign a paper reiterating the pledges made in the treaty of December last,[3] have been

[1]Herrero Delgadito (Little Iron Worker) was a famed chief and ironsmith of the Navajos residing near present-day Wheatfields, Arizona. By the Bonneville Treaty of 1858, Herrero was appointed "Head Chief" of the Navajo Nation.

[2]Zarcillas Largas or Long Earrings, was a famed war chief in his youth, and later gained prominence among his tribesmen as a medicine man and orator. He was killed in October 1860, near the eastern mouth of Cañon de Chelly, by Utes in the employment of Colonel R. E. S. Canby.

[3]On July 14, 1859, Major John S. Simonson held council with Navajo headmen. At this meeting "an article of agreement" was put forward for the signature

actively engaged in bringing in stock as indemnity for property said to have been stolen by Navajos. In fact all the wealthy and influential men of the nation are solicitous for peace and are assisting in restoring the reputed stolen property. Doubtless the present force[4] in their country has done much towards bringing about the present state of feeling existing among them. The *ladrones* (or bad men as they call them) are undoubtedly the thieves and commit the depredations. They have nothing to lose and if war were made upon them now, the innocent and those most active for the preservation of peace would be the sufferers. It is an unquestionable fact that many horses and sheep have been stolen on the frontier and settlements by the Navajos but there is reason to believe that the numbers are very greatly exaggerated; and it is very doubtful if a single murder has been committed by them since the peace of December last. They on the contrary assert that two of their people have been murdered; that many of their horses have been stolen; that they have never been offered restoration for property or people and they claim that their losses

---

of the chiefs. This document was intended, if signed by the Navajos, to bind them to restoration of all property stolen (or its equivalent) since the conclusion of the Bonneville Treaty, as well as that stolen since August 15, 1858. However, Herrero and Zarcillas Largas had seen enough of these pieces of paper, and knew how much reliance Anglos put upon them. They persuaded the other headmen not to sign the "agreement." The chiefs, however, verbally promised to repay all they had stolen. *Annual Report of Commissioners of Indian Affairs* (Washington: 1859), p. 716. Also Baker to Collins, July 17, 1859; *National Archives,* Records of the New Mexico Superintendency of Indian Affairs, Letters received from Agencies, 1859.

[4]At this time there were, besides the regular garrison at Fort Defiance, nearly 700 troops in Navajoland under the command of Major John S. Simonson.

should be taken into account. Another complaint is that their agents (*Tatoes*) are frequently changed before they can become acquainted with them; that from the death of Mr. Dodge[5] to the arrival of Major Baker, no agent apparently took any interest in their affairs. I would state that Major Baker has acquired their confidence and is popular among them.

They have evinced no hostility towards the troops, made no objections to explorations of their country and have furnished guides and information when requested. At this moment they are endeavoring to procure contributions of sheep and horses and say they will indemnify claimants for stolen property as far as they are able. Whatever the offenses of these people may have been heretofore, their present conduct will not justify hostilities against them; I have the concurrence of Major Baker, (their agent) in this opinion.

[5]Henry Linn Dodge, second Navajo Agent, was the son of Senator Henry Dodge of Wisconsin, and brother to Augustus Caesar Dodge, Senator from Missouri. Henry Linn Dodge received his appointment as Indian Agent from President Pierce in August 1853, and replaced Samuel Baird, the first appointee. By natural aptitude and experience, Dodge was an excellent choice. He was a soldier of considerable experience, a veteran of Rocky Mountain exploration and Santa Fe Trail escort; and was with the John M. Washington expedition to Navajoland in 1849. Dodge served as commissary agent for the garrison of U.S. Dragoons stationed at Cebolleta; and at the same time engaged in trading ventures with the Navajos and Pueblo Indians. As Navajo Agent he was considered by these Indians as a trusted friend and was directly responsible for establishing peaceful co-existence between the Navajos, New Mexicans and other neighboring tribes. Unfortunately for Navajo-Anglo relations, Dodge met a tragic death at the hands of Coyotero Apaches in November 1856. For additional information see: Dodge Biographical File in the *Arizona Pioneers' Historical Society,* Tucson, Arizona. Also Dodge's Service Record; *National Archives,* Adjutant General's Office; and J. Buford to L. McLaws, June 1, 1850; *National Archives,* Records of U. S. Army Commands, Department of New Mexico, Record Group 98, Letters Received.

Having reserved the hay ground from which we are now cutting and putting up hay, the grazing in the vicinity of the post has become very short and unless recent rains bring forward the grass rapidly I may be compelled to send the mounted troops to Bear Springs for grazing purposes.

My instructions are to continue explorations until the 15th of September if grass is sufficient, but do not authorize the return of the troops to their several posts at that or any other time. Should the Department Commander deem further operations unnecessary and order for their return is requisite, owing to the want of vegetables, scurvy is becoming prevalent especially among the commands not belonging to the post.

Since my arrival all animals at or in vicinity of this post have been put upon half rations of corn. They receive none when on scouting duties, but even with this reduction, the quantity of corn on hand, including that received by Russell's train[6] this morning, cannot last beyond the 1st of September.

I respectfully add that in consideration of the above facts together with the peaceful disposition of the Indians the knowledge of the country obtained by the explorations and the strength of the permanent garrison of this post, the impeding of the return of the troops to

---

[6]This was U.S. Army quartermaster, Powell Russell, who was killed by Navajos while on his way to Fort Canby (Fort Defiance) on January 3, 1863.

their respective stations is respectively submitted and recommended.

Very respectfully, Sir
Your obt. Servt., etc.

J. S. Simonson
Maj. R. M. R.
Comd. troops in the
Navajo country

1st Lieut. J. D. Wilkens
Assistant Adjutant General
Department of New Mexico
Santa Fé

Casa Blanca, Cañon de Chelly

—*Courtesy Southwest Museum.*

THROUGH CAÑON DE CHELLY

THROUGH CAÑON DE CHELLY

Camp La Joya near Ft. Defiance
August 3, 1859

Sir:

The column placed under my command by Orders No. 8, dated "Head Quarters, Navajo Command, Fort Defiance, N. M., July 14, 1859,"[7] marched from this camp on the morning of the 18th ulto.; and proceeding northward, encamped on the 19th near the head of the Cañon de Chelly about 28 miles north of Fort Defiance. The common belief that it is in this cañon that the Navajos take refuge with their flocks and herds upon the first alarm of war, as well as the extraordinary accounts given of its natural features by the few whites that pretend to have explored it, rendered it highly desirable that this mysterious chasm should be thoroughly explored. That the anxiety of the Indians to maintain their important secret would cause them to resist any attempt on our part to explore the Chelly, although the received opinion, did not

---

[7]A search of army records in the National Archives failed to located Orders No. 8. From references made by Captains J. G. Walker and O. L. Shepherd, it can be concluded that these orders were almost identical to Orders No. 14.

seem probable. At all events I had a force sufficiently strong to disregard such a consideration, and accordingly on the morning of the 20th, having secured the unwilling services of two or three of the principal men of the Navajos as guides and hostages, I set out for the cañon. The unwillingness of the Indians to guide us into it was very decided, arising according to them, from the fact that the descent into the cañon in this direction or vicinity was impracticable for animals with packs, and that if we attempted it, we would lose a large number and might punish or blame them for our disaster. Whatever other cause there might have been for their unwillingness, it is certain that our first view into the cañon was far from being reassuring and seemed to confirm the Indians' statement. While nothing could exceed the terrible grandeur of the view, nothing seemed more impracticable than the descent. The approach of the Chelly, is over an undulating table land, unmarked by any peculiarity, with absolutely nothing to indicate the vicinity of one of the greatest of natural phenomena, until you are startled by finding yourself suddenly upon the brink of this fearful chasm, which seems to open under your very feet into the very bowels of the earth. The cañon is formed by the union of three small streams, the Estrella or Cienega Negra on the southeast, the Pala Negra or more properly the Chelly on the northeast, and the Cienega Juanica on the northwest.[8] The place of our descent is about half a

---

[8] The Rio Estrella or Cienega Negra is present-day Whisky Creek. The Pala Negra is now known as Palisade Creek; and Cienega Juanica is today Wheatfield Creek. All are tributaries of the Rio Chelly, rising in the Chuska-Tunicha Mountains.

mile below the mouth of the last, at a point where the precipice is somewhat broken and the *debris* consisting of immense boulders and disintegrated sandstone give a sufficient slope to enable us to zigzag down the face of the precipice, which at this point cannot be less than six or seven hundred feet high. The process was slow and not unattended with danger to our pack animals, some of which losing their balance were toppled over by the weight of their packs, but the mules' extreme tenacity of life saved us from loss, with the exception of one mule which had a leg broken by the fall and had to be shot. It was four hours before the last of our pack animals reached the bottom and our march resumed.

From its head to its mouth the cañon runs nearly west, and its width is from two hundred to three hundred and fifty yards, seldom less than the one or greater than the other. As we proceeded down the cañon we found the bluffs to increase in height, being generally mural and perpendicular and of about equal altitude on opposite sides. Being composed of sandstone exclusively, in many places the elements have converted them into gigantic cathedrals, fortifications, castles, etc., or what the fancy might easily convert into such when seen at a distance. The soil of the cañon valley is extremely sandy but supports a growth of underbrush and is not without fertility, as numerous patches of corn thoughout the cañon and an occasional one of wheat indicate. Copious rains having fallen during the last few days, we found running water through the entire length of the cañon, but during the dry season water is only found by digging in the dry and sandy bed of the arroyo, as the Indians informed us. The first side cañon entering the Chelly is from the south[9] and joins the Chelly ten or eleven miles from where we entered it, and is the same by which Col. Miles entered the Chelly in November last, during the Navajo war.[10] The Indians call it by a name which our Mexican interpreter said signifies *Alsada* or the the Cañon of High Rock from a lofty and spire-like pillar at its mouth, which detached entirely from the neighboring precipice and with a base of not more than one or two hundred feet, rises perpendicularly to the height of seven or eight hundred feet and terminating in a sharp steeple-like point, near which on a narrow ledge grows a cedar tree.[11] Nothing can exceed the grandeur of the scenery of this part of the cañon where the precipices reach their greatest elevation, which is probably not far from one thousand feet, but having no means of accurate measurement this is conjectural.

Just before going into camp this morning, one mile below the mouth of Cañon Alsada, on the only spot of grass we had seen in the cañon, we were overtaken by a thunderstorm and a deluge of rain, but the temporary inconvenience caused by this was amply conpensated for by the novel and beautiful sight of a waterfall of nearly a

---

[9]This is present-day Monument Cañon.

[10]Here Walker is wrong. In November 1858 Colonel Miles' command skirted the rim of Cañon del Muerto, and arrived at a point near present-day Chinle. It was on September 11 that Miles, with a force of Mounted Riflemen and Third Infantrymen, was led into Monument Cañon by Blas Lucero, a New Mexican guide from Albuquerque.

[11]"The lofty and spire-like pillar," rising 400 feet above the cañon floor is sacred to the Navajos, who call it, *Tsena'asdj'ih,* Spider Rock. It is said that Spider Woman once wove her web over this pinnacle.

thousand feet in perpendicular height, from the table-land above to the bottom of the cañon.

The volume of water was considerable, but after falling some hundreds of feet it was broken into a lace-like sheet of pure white which swayed back and forth with the wind; a little further down it became spray and finally reached the bottom as fine mist. Resuming our march the next morning we found the cañon and overhanging precipices presenting the same general features, but the line of mural precipices is more frequently broken by short lateral openings, but none of them exceeding a few hundred yards in length. The only exception to this is the entrance from the north of the Cañon del Trigo or Wheat Cañon,[12] which joins the Chelly about three miles from the mouth of the latter. The Navajos say it rises in the Tunicha Mountains to the northeast and is inhabited and cultivated.

About a mile and a half above the mouth of the Trigo we stopped to examine the ruins of an ancient pueblo,[13] built partly at the base of the cliff and partly on a ledge

-----

[12]This is Cañon del Muerto which did not receive its modern name until after 1886, when the archaeological expedition of James Stevenson discovered many remains of the prehistoric inhabitants of the cañon.

[13]Walker is referring to that 13th century cliff dwelling, known today as White House Ruin. Located some two miles above the fork of the main cañon, this ruin derives its name from a yellowish-white room perched high above the ruin proper. Divided into sections, this unusual and extensive pueblo attracted the attention of nearly every visitor to Cañon de Chelly. It was sketched in 1849 by Edward M. Kern, artist to the expedition of Col. John M. Washington. In 1893 Cosmos Mindelieff, archaeologist for the Smithsonian Institution, performed the first scientific investigation of the ruin; and it was he who labeled it "Casa Blanca." Thirty years later Earl Morris, sponsored by the Carnegie Institute, carried on further excavations at the site.

forty or fifty feet from the ground. The building on the ground seems to have been a large quadrangular structure, divided into numerous apartments, with doors, windows and fireplaces not unlike those of civilized nations. At one end of the building and within the *encente* is the *estufa* or place of scared fire, similar in size and form to that at the ruined pueblo on the Pecos River twenty-five miles from Santa Fe.[14] The buildings in the rocks are in an almost perfect state of preservation, even to the wooden supports of the doors and windows and the white-wash on the exterior walls which look new and fresh as if placed there within the year. This would seem to argue no great antiquity of origin, but their perfect state of preservation is owing to their being protected by the overhanging precipices in such a manner that rain has never reached them. I regretted exceedingly that we had no means of reaching these buildings and of examining more closely these remains of an ancient and perhaps extinct race.

That the builders of these houses had made considerable progress in the civilized arts is apparent from the superior style of masonry and earthernware vessels,

------

[14]Walker is referring to Pecos Pueblo which was finally abandoned about 1832. Abraham R. Johnston, a member of Doniphan's Army during the Mexican War, described this ruined pueblo in his journal: "We encamped near the ruins of old Pecos village, a curious relic of the Montezuma race, consisting of the ruins of an extensive range of buildings covering ten or fifteen acres. Here the sacred fire was kept burning until within a few years. It stands on a semicircular ledge of rocks, which rise about fifty feet above the general level in an irregular plain of several miles wide between the mountains. The buildings were of small stones rudely laid up with mud, and some of the walls [are] of unburnt brick . . . ." Abraham R. Johnston, *Marching with the Army of the West*, edited by Ralph P. Bieber (Glendale: Arthur H. Clark, 1936), p. 102.

fragments of which we found about these ruins. The Navajos say that their ancestors found these ruins just as they now appear when they first came to the country; notwithstanding it seems almost certain that the builders and inhabitants of these houses were the peaceful and unwarlike Moquis,[15] whom the more warlike and numerous Navajos expelled to the country fifty miles to the southward, where they still live. The perfect identity in the style and situation of their buildings—the character of their masonry and pottery, and more than all the universal *estufa,* formed at these ruined pueblos and in the Moqui villages leave no ground of doubt that the builders of these ancient pueblos and the Moqui Indians are one and the same race. That they were at one period the predominant race throughout New Mexico, seems equally certain from the uniform character of the ruins on both sides of the Rio Grande. There are several other ruins of a similar character further down the cañon, but less extensive and in a less perfect state of preservation. A short distance below the ruined pueblo just spoken of, we observed an Indian ascending what appeared in the distance to be the face of a perpendicular bluff, but on a nearer approach we found the bluff slightly receding and that there was a flight of steps cut in the solid rock from the bottom to the top, perhaps six or seven hundred feet high. Lower down we observed several other flights on each side of the cañon all of which were probably the work of a more ancient race than the present inhabitants.

———

[15]Hopis.

The bluffs which have all this day's march been growing gradually less imposingly lofty, below the mouth of
the Trigo three and a half miles from the mouth of the
Chelly, rapidly sink until they finally disappear entirely
and the undulating country beyond presents a barren
and uninviting appearance with ranges of mountains in
the distance to the southwest and northeast.

From our camp near the mouth of the Cañon Alsada
to where the Chelly frees itself from the cañon and turns
due north, is about nine and a half miles—the portion
of the cañon explored the day before, about twelve miles,
making the distance traveled in the cañon the two days,
twenty one and a half miles. I will here remark, that
twelve days afterwards, when returning from the Rio
San Juan to this camp, we encamped early in the after-
noon on the Pala Negra or Chelly Creek, the central or
eastern branch of the Chelly, near where we had encamped on the 19th before descending into the Chelly.
Thinking that possibly the Indian had taken me by the
most difficult route to deter other parties of our troops
from attempting on any further occasion to go into the
cañon. I took a party of riflemen on foot and accompanied
by Lieut. DuBois[16] descended the cañon about three and

---

[16]John Van Dusen DuBois was a native of New York, and graduated from
West Point on July 1, 1851. As an officer of the Regiment of Mounted Rifles,
he participated in overland trail duty, as well as several campaigns against the
Apaches and Navajo Indians. With the outbreak of the Civil War, DuBois remained loyal to the Union; and was transferred to the Third Cavalry in August
1861; and a month later to the Missouri Light Artillery. Attainment of rank,
however, seemed to have been slow for this officer, for close of the Civil War
found him only with the rank of major. DuBois remained in the army until 1876,
retiring from active duty in May of that year.

a half miles, examining the mouth of the Cienega Negra or southeastern branch of the Cañon, which enters about three miles below what might be termed the heart of the Chelly, and then descended to near the mouth of the Cienega Juanica and within half a mile of the point where we entered the Chelly on the 20th, thus completing the reconnaissance of the heretofore mysterious cañon, which we find to be about twenty-four or twenty-five miles in length, and running nearly due west almost on a straight line. Although the head and mouth of the cañon had previously been fixed by astronomical observations, the exaggerated length given heretofore to it, arose from an erroneous curve [to] the southward as laid down on all the conjectural maps of the cañon.

There is, we found, no descent into the cañon by this last explored route that can at all be considered practicable for animals. In regard to the road by which we descended on the 20th, there is a trail on the opposite side of the cañon and a little above where we entered it leading to the table land above by which animals *without* packs might ascend or descend, but I doubt if they could do either with them. Our reconnaissance of the Chelly I think explodes the notion so long prevalent, that it could afford a refuge for the Navajos, and their numerous flocks and herds for any length of time in a war with us.[17] The destitution of pasturage in the cañon would it-

----

[17]Walker is referring to the notion, so long prevalent among Spanish and subsequent Mexican regimes in New Mexico, that this vast cañon system was an impregnable stronghold of the Navajos during times of war. Actually, Navajo flocks and herds were grazed along the cañon rims, and portions of the river bed below, reserved for agriculture.

self force them out. Besides, now that the Navajos are aware of our acquaintance with the Chelly, it is not probable that any number of them would rely upon it in time of war as a place of concealment and refuge. Should they do so, a column of mounted men in the cañon, supported if thought necessary by a flanking force of infantry on the table [to] the east of the mouth of the Trigo, and to the north of the Chelly would in two days time sweep the cañon from one end to the other.[18] A thorough examination of the side of the cañons of the Chelly would have been desirable, particularly of the Trigo, of which nothing is known, but the several days necessary for the purpose, with my limited supply of provisions, might have prevented me from carrying out Major Simonson's instructions to extend my explorations as far as the San Juan, and of "visiting the various bands of Indians" on my route, and of noting their numbers, locations, herds of horses and cattle, flocks of sheep and goats, as well as their grazing grounds in summer and winter; watering places, and in general, everything that might become useful in case of war. On that account I determined to reach the Rio San Juan at the nearest point from the mouth of the Chelly Cañon, and afterwards return to

---

[18]Walker was not the first military man to make this tactical observation. In September 1849 Lieutenant James H Simpson, while accompanying the John M. Washington expedition noted: "Should it be necessary to send troops into this cañon . . . a force should skirt the heights above to drive off assailants from that quarter, the south bank should be preferred, because [it is] less interrupted by lateral branch cañons." These were exactly the tactics used by Colonel Christopher "Kit" Carson and his First New Mexico Volunteers during the Navajo roundup in February 1864. James H. Simpson, *Journal of a Military Reconnaissance, from Santa Fe to the Navajo Country* (Philadelphia: 1852), pp. 73-77.

Fort Defiance across the Tunicha Mountains by a trail yet untravelled by our troops, or exploring parties which was described by my interpreter as being a good road and with an abundance of water and grass.

How I carried out this part of my instructions will probably be better shown by extracting from my journal the notes herewith subjoined:—

JULY 22.—Left camp at 7 o'clock this morning and following the Rio Chelly which after freeing itself from the cañon turns due north,[19] for six miles we passed a succession of fields of growing corn, some of them containing from forty to sixty acres.[20] This valley and the lower half of the cañon are probably the most populous portions of the Navajo country. They have but few herds of sheep and consequently considered poor, living principally by agriculture. They seem very unwarlike and well disposed towards us, but upon them the chief burden of war with us would fall, for the destruction of their growing corn would reduce them to starvation and extreme misery, although their peaceful habits, and remoteness from our settlements make it probable that they have been entirely guiltless of any offenses. The last cultivated land we saw upon the Chelly is almost six miles from the mouth of the cañon, and the Indians informed us that there was no cultivation lower down, but that the country is grazed over a good deal in the fall,

---

[19]Present-day Chinle Wash.

[20]This area along the alluvial flats of Chinle Wash has always been prime agricultural land to the Navajos; and today is known as "Many Farms."

after the rains have brought up the gramma grass upon the plains.

Our guides say, that our course today and tomorrow lays along the Rio Chelly, but owing to the recent heavy rains to avoid the quicksand it will be advisable to leave the river valley, and turn off to the right, across the mesa. While halting for noon we had a heavy rain upon us, and upon resuming our march found the road extremely heavy. Our course today has been north—camped near some dark blue clay mounds—rain water in arroyo, very little grass. Distance marched today, seventeen miles.

JULY 23.—Our course today north. About six miles from camp passed a peculiar house looking isolated—red bluff at the southwest, corner of which there is an opening resembling a window. Ten miles from camp reached an arroyo generally dry, as the guides say, but now with running water. Here we crossed Major Backus' trail of last October.[21] After following the arroyo about a mile halted for noon, and resuming our march at 3 o'clock followed down the arroyo a mile and a half and within sight of the Rio Chelly. Five miles from the arroyo passed to the right of an isolated rock called by the

---

[21]During the Navajo War of 1858 a column of troops under the command of Major Electus Backus, consisting of companies E and G, Mounted Riflemen, Company D, Third Infantry; and B, I, and E, Eighth Infantry, rendezvoused at the Pueblo of Jemez in mid-Ocober. Marching from Jemez, Backus' troops made their way to the valley of Tunicha, thence through Cañon Blanco, passed through Washington Pass and skirted the eastern slopes of the Tunicha Mountains, and united with troops under command of Colonel Dixon Miles. The combined force then struck westward, passing over the northern rim of Cañon de Chelly.

Mexicans "Piedra Rodia,"[22] then ascending a sharp hill reached a spring in the hills a mile and a half beyond. We have had a very sandy country to pass over today, and the march has been very trying on our animals, particularly the pack mules. Day's march, eighteen miles.

JULY 24.—For a mile and a half after leaving camp our road led due east to the top of a rocky ridge, where there is for a mile or more a natural pavement, and where we found pools of rain water. For four miles the trail is over a sandy mesa to a rocky arroyo with rain water in pools, where we nooned, after which we marched east of north five and a half miles to an arroyo with rain water in holes. Grass good. Day's march twelve miles.

JULY 25.—Course from camp N.E. to the extreme western point of the mountains—seven miles to a wide plain, after which course turns more towards the north, say N. 20° E. and continued in this direction for eight miles to permanent running water and good grass. Day's march, fifteen miles.

JULY 26.—Course from camp north—three miles to a cottonwood grove called "Bosque Redondo" where there is permanent water and good grass. Seven miles over a rocky and hilly country to the Rio San Juan. Went up the river one mile and camped on tolerable grass. Day's march, eleven miles.

The San Juan, which I had before seen as a clear and beautiful stream is now so muddy that even the animals

---

[22]Probably Round Rock, a high isolated sandstone mesa in two section, located eighteen miles north of Chinle.

refuse to drink it. The guides say that the Arroyos Tunicha and Colorado above, which usually send no water to the San Juan, swollen by the late heavy rains are now running out into the river and defiling its waters. By digging holes in the sand near the edge of the water we procured pure water for drinking.

JULY 27.—Remained in camp on the river.

JULY 28.—Followed up the course of the river for ten miles to the mouth of the Arroyo Colorado, by a very hilly and bad road. Five miles below the mouth of the Colorado there is excellent grass on the river bottom. At the mouth of the Arroyo Colorado we nooned and afterwards turned up it and leaving the San Juan followed it for nine miles due south, where we encamped—grass poor—water in holes which the guides say is permanent. Day's march, nineteen miles.

JULY 29.—After leaving camp travelled three miles due south to a point from which the "Needles" or "Sierra Aguila" as it is variously called bore due east and about three miles distant. A little further on came to a cross trail coming from the direction of the "Needles" and into this we turned against the advice of our Indian guides who insisted that the better road lay further east, but as I had to be constantly on my guard against their misrepresentations, made in order to take us by routes the least frequented by Indians and their herds, I did not follow their advice. (My subsequent experience of the superiority of this route and of its being the great thoroughfare of the Navajos from one side of the mountains to the other convinced me that my suspicions had been well founded.)

Following this cross trail three miles up a sandy arroyo, course S. 25° W., we emerged upon a wide plain extending to the base of the mountain, which at the point at which we are approaching it bends towards the south, leaving this plain called "Mesa Colorado,"[23] lying within the crescent. This extended plain is an important grazing ground for sheep and horses in the fall of the year, after the rains have brought up the gramma grass. The grazing, even now, is tolerable and in a few weeks will be excellent. Six miles across the mesa, crossing Major Backus' trail of October last, we encamped near some red rocks with rain water in arroyo. To the eastward of us is a peculiar pillar-like rock standing isolated on the plain.[24] The guides report permanent water at several places near our camp, and although the constant and heavy rain more than supplied all our wants, yet I have no doubt but that all seasons a sufficient supply could be found between the mountains and the San Juan. The constant rain we have had, adding as it does so materially to the weight of the tracks together with the bad water and deep sandy road are telling on our mules, and two were so much exhausted on the road today that they could not be brought into camp and were consequently shot by the rear guard. Day's march, fourteen miles. Grass at camp good.

_____

[23]Mesa Colorado, now known as Red Rock Valley, is an area of broken red sandstone country linking the Lukachukai and Carrizo Mountains.

[24]Standing Red Rock is a sandstone crag surmounted by a rock resembling a teakettle. It is situated in the middle of Red Rock Valley.

JULY 30.—Course today S. 15° W. over a broken and hilly country intersected by arroyos. Five miles from camp permanent water and Navajo corn fields with quite a number of huts, but uninhabited—the people have left this side of the mountain from fear of the Utahs, who we were told, recently drove off a *caballado* of 80 horses from the neighborhood.[25] Seven miles from camp commenced to ascend the mountains—half mile up an excellent spring—two miles to the summit where there is another spring of ice cold water. Half mile further, on the top of the mountain, a small lake. The road up the mountain is steep but infinitely superior to that by which Major Simonson's command crossed the mountains about a month ago. Besides, the mountains at this point seem of about half the elevation of that part crossed by Major Simonson's command, and I am convinced from the appearance of the road that it is the main thoroughfare of the Navajos across the mountains, although they may be crossed at almost any point, if it were necessary. From the lake we commenced gradually to descend by a good and much travelled trail which follows the course of the wooded ravine, with a stream of clear water running through it and its volume constantly increased by springs breaking out along the sides of the

---

[25]This area had always been a scene of trouble between Utes and Navajos. In February 1857, Utes raided between the northern point of the Tunichas and the eastern mouth of Cañon de Chelly. Eight Navajos were killed during these forays; and the tribe retaliated by slaying five Utes north of the Rio San Juan. From then until the time of Walker's reconnaissance, a state of war existed between the two tribes. See Capt. H. L. Kendrick to Maj. William A. Nichols, February 11, 1857; *National Archives*, Department of New Mexico, Record Group 98, Letters Received.

mountains. From Washington's Pass[26] to the Carizo [*sic*] range,[27] the Tunicha Mountains might be compared to an open hand, the fingers separated. The back of the hand with the knuckles vertical would represent the northern slope and the highest ridge—the fingers a series of lateral spurs running off toward the south and tapering down towards the plains, and the space between the fingers, the wooded ravines and fertile and well watered valleys that abound through these mountains, which afford excellent summer pasturage for great numbers of horses and sheep. Nine miles from the top of the mountains we came to a large Cienega at "the Junta de las Arroyos." Here we encamped. Day's march, twenty miles.

JULY 31.—Course still down the Arroyo Tusa, S. 5° West, for six miles when we emerged from the mountains and left the creek, turning S. 15° E. around a peculiar pillar-like rock which bears from our camp this evening at Pala Negra, N. 10° W. Ten miles further (crossing the "Monton la Jara" and the "Cienega Juanica") we reached our camp of the 19th and encamped a half mile beyond at a good spring with tolerable grass on the Cienega. Day's march, sixteen miles.

---

[26]Washington Pass, also known as Cottonwood Pass, is the high mountain divide separating the Tunicha and Chuska Mountains. It is named in honor of Colonel John M. Washington, Military Governor of New Mexico, who in 18.9, passed over a Navajo trail from present-day Sheep Springs westward to the vicinity of Crystal.

[27]The pine and spruce covered Carrizo Mountains are located in the extreme northern corner of the state of Arizona. The range is shown as the Sierra de Chegui on the Dominguez-Escalante map of 1776; and as the Sierra de Carriso on the map prepared by J. F. McComb in 1860.

(In these notes I have given the course according to the true north and not the *Magnetic North,* the latter being about 10° eastwards.)

AUGUST 1.—Reached this camp by way of "Cienega Negra." The country to the south of the Tunicha Mountains is swarming with horses and sheep driven in by their fears of the Utahs. In regard to cattle, very few of the Navajos have them, at least I have seen none. Day's march, twenty one miles.

Before closing the report I would remark that the Navajos everywhere evinced the most earnest desire for peace. I am not prepared to say what would be the better tone of policy towards them, but there is no doubt that a war made upon them now by us would fall heaviest upon the least guilty—would transform a nation which has already made considerable progress in civilized arts into a race of beggars, vagabonds and robbers.

What consideration such views should have on the settlement of our difficulties with them—difficulties based upon exaggerated demands—which every animal in the Navajo country would scarcely be sufficient to satisfy, it is not for one to suggest, but before severe measures are resolved on and a course of policy initiated that would entail poverty and wretchedness upon the entire tribe, it may be that some little forbearance might be the part of true wisdom.

Accompanying this will be found a topographical sketch of the route travelled over by the column under my command by Lieut. DuBois which I have carefully examined and found accurate in every respect. Perfect accuracy of course is unattainable without the use of instruments for determining latitude and longitude which he did not possess.

> I am Sir,
> Very Respectfully,
>> J. G. WALKER
>> Capt. R. M. R.
>> Comdg. 2d. Col. Nav. Com'd.

Headqrs. Dept. of New Mex.
August 31, 1859

Official
John D. Wilkins
1st Lieut., 3rd Infantry
Asst. Adjt. Genl.

The Moqui Pueblos

Courtesy Southwest Museum

TO THE PUEBLOES OF MOQUI

TO THE PUEBLOS OF MOQUI

Fort Defiance, N. M.
August 7, 1859

SIR:

I have the honor respectfully to report that in compliance with Orders No. 8, dated Head Quarters Navajo Command, Fort Defiance, N.M., July 14, 1856, I proceeded with companies B, K, and detachment Company I, 3rd Infantry, commanded by Lieut. Dickinson[28] and Capt. Sykes,[29] and Lieut. Greerley,[30] 3rd Inf., and com-

---

[28]A native of Connecticut, William Dickinson was not a West Point graduate but rose, instead, through the ranks. On February 21, 1857, he was commissioned a second lieutenant in the Third Infantry; and served in New Mexico until outbreak of the Sectional Controversy. Unlike many officers of his day, Dickinson remained loyal to the Union; and received a brevet major on July 21, 1861, for gallant and meritorious conduct at the Battle of Bull Run.

[29]George Sykes of Maryland graduated from West Point in July 1838, and began his duty with the Third Infantry. During the Mexican War his conduct was conspicuous, and on April 18, 1847, he was breveted captain for gallant and meritorious conduct at the Battle of Cerro Gordo. Following his frontier duty in New Mexico, Sykes quickly rose in rank, retiring as a major general after the Civil War.

[30]This may be a misprint in the original text, as no Lieutenant Greerley is listed on Army rosters and directories. There is, however, a Henry William Freedley listed for the same regiment (Third Infantry). Freedley graduated from West Point in July 1851, and immediately began his duty on the western fron-

panies G and K, Mounted Riflemen commanded by Lieu-
tenants Edson[31] and Claflin,[32] Regiment Rifles, on the
18th ultimo, to examine the country lying west and southwest of this fort.

On the 18th and 19th July the line of march was for
30 miles over the Moqui wagon road leading hence to
the Indian pueblo of Moqui; also for 6 miles on the 20th
of July. As the region immediately along this road is so
well known, nothing special or new can be offered. After
leaving the Moqui road on the 20th, the line of march
was about south for 7 miles, till we reached the Rio
Pueblitos on which we encamped the night previous.
Water not permanent. On the 21st our route ran southwest through the Cañon of the Rio Pueblito for 15 miles.
Water not permanent.

JULY 22.—The route was west for 10 miles, into a large
cañada leading west in the direction of the Moqui villages; no trail. Water not permanent.

The guides, Juan and José, not knowing that section
of the country, it was thought best not to pursue this
valley any further, fearing a want of water for as large a
number of animals as were in the command, therefore on

---

tier. With the outbreak of the Civil War, he served conspicuously throughout
the conflict, receiving brevet commissions after the battles of Chancellorsville
and Gettysburg.

[31]John Henry Edson of New York graduated from West Point in July 1848;
and immediately began his frontier duty with the Mounted Rifles. He remained
in New Mexico until outbreak of the Civil War, at which time he transferred to
the First Massachusetts Cavalry, and later to the Tenth Vermont Infantry.

[32]Ira Wallace Claflin of Vermont, also a West Point graduate (class of 1853),
began his frontier duty in New Mexico; and served throughout the Confederate
invasion of that territory. He received a brevet captaincy for gallant conduct dur-
the Battle of Valverde.

on the 23rd July the direction of the Ojo de la Jarra,[33] on the Moqui road, was taken and this spring was reached in about 15 miles. Water permanent. No trail and hilly. The 24th, 25th and 26th were occupied in travelling over the Moqui road till reaching these Indian towns, about 30 miles. This part of the route being so well known; nothing new be offered. On the way of reaching these Indian pueblos, three of them, viz., Anoche, Shuehomobe, and Walbe were visited by the officers.[34]

JULY 27.—We marched for better grass further west about 6 miles, in front of the two Pueblos of Muchonobe and Chupaulebe,[35] which were also visited the same day by a portion of the officers. Encamped at rain water ponds.

JULY 28.—We marched 5 miles further west and north west of the Pueblo of Thomopebe. Encamped at rain water ponds. This pueblo and Oryebe lying 15 miles north[36] were visited by myself and Lieut. Greerley and Claflin. This day the chief of Chupalebe and a head man of Thomopebe promised to lead us for two days south.

JULY 29.—We marched 15 miles south and encamped in the same cañada that we left on the 23rd. Water

---

[33]Ojo de la Jarra is probably the Senatoa Springs shown on the map of the Navajo Country prepared by the late Herbert Gregory.

[34]The three Hopi pueblos which Capt. Shepherd is referring to are: Hano, Sichomovi, and Walpi—all are situated on East or First Mesa.

[35]Shepherd's spelling of these Hopi villages is phonetical and corresponds to Mishongnovi and Shipaulovi. Both are situated on Middle or Second Mesa.

[36]Shepherd's command is near Third Mesa, and he is referring to Oraibi and probably Shungopovi (on Second Mesa).

not permanent. July 30th we marched still south for about 12 miles, and encamped on the southern side of some black and high mesas, from which could be seen the Rio Colorado Chiquito,[37] and supposed to be about 20 miles distant and further south. Here we have but little water for the animals. Water permanent.

JULY 31.—We marched in direction of E.S.E. thru a broad range of high and large black mesas, sufficiently detached to leave beautiful valleys between; distance is say about 20 miles, and no trail. Water not permanent.

AUGUST 1.—Marched east for about 10 miles and encamped on the Rio Pueblitos[38] and no trail. Water not permanent.

AUGUST 2.—Marched E.S.E. for 15 miles to another Ojo de la Jarra, on the Zuni and Moqui trail. Water permanent and abundant.

AUGUST 3.—Marched E.N.E. for 14 miles, when we reached the ruins of Pueblo Grande, thence marched E.S.E. for 4 miles and encamped on top of the mountain at the tanks of the Agua and Viberas. Water not permanent.

AUGUST 4.—Marched E.S.E. for 15 miles when we entered the lower end of the Cañon de Calites,[39] and thence

[37]Little Colorado River.

[38]Rio Pueblitos or Pueblo Colorado Wash rises at nearly 8500 feet from the western slopes of the Defiance Plateau.

[39]Today Cañon de Calites is known as Black Creek, and heads on the western slopes of the Chuska Mountains and the Defiance Plateau. The Creek runs in a southerly direction and joins the Rio Puerco of the West, one-half mile south of Houck, Arizona.

turned up in direction of N.N.E. for 3 miles. Encamped at the mouth of cañon. Water not permanent.

AUGUST 5.—Marched through the Cañon of the Calites after much labor and difficulty; Cañon for about 6 miles being choked up with a dense growth of undergrowth and willow; the ground besides being miry in many places from recent rains. This cañon has never been entirely traversed before. Encamped in the upper Cañon of the Calites, distance 20 miles and direction about N.E. Water near camp permanent.

AUGUST 6.—The command marched to this post 10 miles making a total distance of about 205 miles.

Reporting the character of the route, I have had to state that the whole distance traversed south of the Moqui wagon road is impracticable, except during the rainy season and it was only in consequence of the previous heavy rains which determined me to march over the route indicated. We saw no Indian along the route except in the Rio Pueblitos the second day out. Near the Moqui villages some 2 or 3 Indians came into camp, but they did not live near there. At the mouth or lower end of the Cañon de Calites, some few came into camp, principally women; also at the tanks near Pueblo Grande.[40] At the last camp in the Cañon of the Calites some few also came into camp. None however, at any point, of a character to hold a talk with. No flocks of sheep were

---

[40]Pueblo Grande was the Spanish designation for the 13th century Anasazi ruin, today known as Wide Ruins. This site is located seventeen miles north of Chambers, on U.S. Highway 66.

seen on the whole route. At the last, only 10 miles from the post, a herd of horses were seen.

Corn fields were seen on the Rio Pueblitos about 30 miles hence, also a few small fields down the Cañon of the Pueblitos on the 4th day out. No fields were thence discovered till we came to the Cañon of the Pueblo Grande, about 30 miles hence S.W.; thence none till we entered the lower end of the Cañon of the Calites where [there] were extensive fields, distance thence about 35 miles, and also in the upper Cañon of the Calites, 16 miles. Some few other patches were seen along the way hardly worth mentioning. Scarcely 100 acres in all were discovered.

Evidence were discovered of wintering large herds of horses and flocks of sheep in the Cañada leaving west towards Moqui, from the lower end of the Cañon of the Rio Pueblitos, as well as in the mesas adjoining this cañon. Also in the Canada of the Ojo de la Jarra near Moqui, and thence particularly in the valley reaching from the Ojo de la Jarra on the Zuñi and Moqui trail, to the Pueblo Grande, and likewise at the lower end of the Cañon of the Calites. In all these places, it must have been warm and sheltered from cold winds, and with grass abundant. The recent rains have caused the grass to spring forth sufficiently to furnish fair grazing; ten days earlier than the expedition started, no grass could have been found.

The expedition has been remarkably successful in having traversed a section of country never before known or attempted, and in demonstrating the possibility of troops going to the remotest haunts of the Indian. Also in having discovered the valley of the Pueblo Grande, so near this post, and hitherto unknown, and where large numbers of Indians must have been during the past severe winter, as indicated by the newness and number of the lodges. Likewise in having penetrated through its whole extent, the Cañon of the Calites, sometimes called the *Chiney* or *Chenay.* All the Indians whom we saw, came into camp freely, and manifested a very friendly disposition.

Regarding the Moqui Indians, they appear to be an honest and very industrious and simple minded people, living almost entirely by cultivating the soil. They have large and flourishing fields of corn. A thousand acres or so came under my own eye, perhaps there were more. It is a well settled fact from the best information, that the Navajo Indians live a great deal upon them; and what they don't sponge they rob, as is evident from there being no horses among them. These Pueblos merit care and protection. The large mountain lying S.W. of the Moqui villages is doubtless the Sierra de Francisco[41] and is beyond the Rio Colorado Chiquito; being about 4 days beyond and the home of the Coninas Indians.[42] I am satisfied that the Navajos never go there to secret themselves or property.

---

[41]San Francisco Peaks near present-day Flagstaff, Arizona.

[42]Coninas are the Havasupai, living in present-day Cataract Cañon. According to the late Richard Van Valkenburgh, the word "Conina or Konina" is a Hopi word of "obscure origin."

The sketch of the route made by Lieut. W. H. Bell, 3rd Infantry, who accompanied the command for that purpose, is respectfully enclosed.

During my station at this post for six years past I have never known a more pacific disposition manifested by the Navajos, and the salutary effect of these explorations is apparent, and has, I think, provided this desired result.

Very Respectfully,

Your obedient servant

O. L. SHEPHERD
Capt. 3rd Infty. Bvt. Major
Comd. Expedition

John D. Wilkins
Lieut. 3rd Infantry
Asst. Adjt. Genl.

P.S.: I forgot to mention that the horses and pack mules returned from the expedition in fair condition notwithstanding the softness of the ground caused by the heavy rains for the first ten days, and the unnutritioness [sic] of the young grass. Only one pack mule was lost, owing to a heavy storm and boggy ground while in marsh.

Santa Fe, August 31, 1859
H. Qrs. Dept. of New Mex.

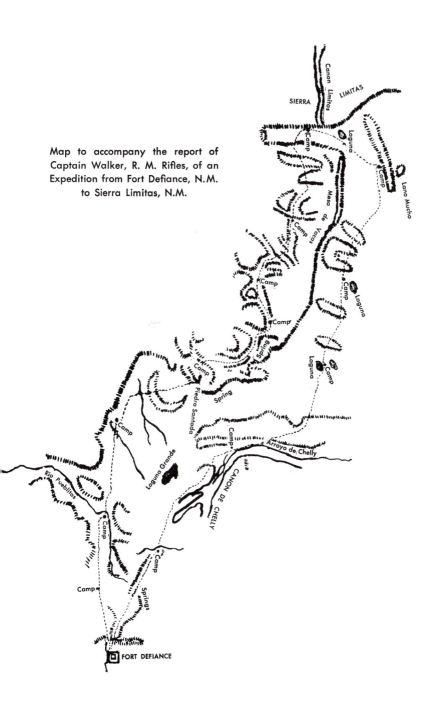

Map to accompany the report of Captain Walker, R. M. Rifles, of an Expedition from Fort Defiance, N.M. to Sierra Limitas, N.M.

SIERRA

Canon Limitas

LIMITAS

Camp

Laguna

Camp

Llano Mucho

Mesa de Vacas

Camp

Camp

Camp

Laguna

Camp

Camp

Laguna

Spring

Laguna

Camp

Piedra Santada

Spring

Camp

Arroyo de Chelly

Camp

Laguna Grande

CAÑON DE CHELLY

Rio Pueblitos

Camp

Camp

Camp

Springs

Camp

FORT DEFIANCE

ORDERS NUMBER 14

Head Quarters, Navajo Command
Fort Defiance, N. M.
September 1, 1869

I. Two columns will leave this post on the 5th instant, each carrying 20 days' rations. The 1st column under command of Bvt. Major O. S. Shepherd, 3rd Infantry, consisting of Company B and Capt. Sykes' command (K and Detachment I) Third Infantry, and Company H and Detachment G, Mounted Rifles; the second column under command of Captain J. G. Walker, R.M.R., consisting of companies C and G, 3rd Infantry and Company K and Detachment E, Mounted Rifles.

II. Major Shepherd's column will march to Chusca Valley, thence east to San Mateo Mountain, thence to the Rio Gallo, thence west side of the Sierra Acoma to the trail leading from Acoma to the Rita Quemado and down that stream one or two days' march, thence returning by way of Zuñi or such other route as Major Shepherd may deem best to obtain knowledge of the country and Indian locations.

III. Capt. Walker's command will march to the Mesa de la Vaca, thence to the Mesa Calabaza and to a mountain beyond, supposed to be southwest, where it is reported there are numerous cañons well watered, and where many Navajos reside with their flocks and herds. It is desirable that these cañons be thoroughly examined. Capt. Walker will exercise his discretion in returning, endeavoring as much as possible to avoid routes heretofore explored.

Lieut. Bell, 3rd Infantry is assigned to this column as Topographical Engineer.

IV. The columns will visit all bands of Navajos in their respective routes, noting their locations, numbers of herds of horses and cattle, flocks of sheep and goats, as well as their grazing grounds and everything useful in case of war. A kind and gentle course will be pursued towards them, at the same time making them understand that it is the determination to become acquainted with their country.

V. Persons and property of all peaceable Indians will be respected—their lodgings or dwellings unmolested. Should depredators or stolen property be surrendered, or captured, such persons and property will be secured.

VI. Acting Assistant Surgeon Bill will accompany Major Major Shepherd's command.

VII. Lieut. Shipley A.A.Q.M. of this post, will furnish pack mules and pack saddles, completely equipped, for that portion of the troops which accompany the columns from this post, in proportion of one to every officer and one to every three men.

VIII. Commanders of columns are authorized to employ a guide and interpreter each.

IX. Reports, accompanied by a sketch of the routes passed over, will be made [to] these Head Quarters by the commanders of columns on their return.

Regards of Maj. Simonson,

J. W. EDSON
2nd Lieut. R. M. R.
Adj. Navj. Command

INTRODUCTORY LETTER

Head Quarters,
Navajo Command
Fort Defiance, N. M.
September 23rd, 1859

Sir:

I have the honor to forward the report and sketch of exploration made by Captain J. G. Walker, R.M.R., in pursuance with Orders No. 14, from these Head Quarters. This report will be found highly useful and interesting having been made over a country heretofore unknown to our troops. The immense coal-beds discovered are of great importance, in view of future railroad construction, being nearly intermediate between the Mississippi and Pacific termini.

Also herewith is forwarded the Special Report of Captain Walker in relation to the movements of the Mormons with the Indian tribes. Not a doubt exists that this tampering with the Indians is to the prejudice of the citizens of the United States, and the intent of the Government.

A Pah-Ute who visited the Indian agent here, informed me of the proposed council at Sierra Panoche and expressed himself anxious to attend it in order (as he says) to bring about a peace with the Navajos. He said the Mormons had baptized him into their church, and gave him a paper certifying he was a Latter-day-Saint, and a good man. He was informed that the President of the United States appointed agents to whose care the interests of the Indian tribes are entrusted, and that all persons assuming these duties without his authority were bad men; that last year the conduct of the Mormons was such that he sent his troops against them, and that now those bad men were endeavoring to get our red brothers identified in their difficulties and troubles. Much more was said of the same tendency, and he promised he would not attend the Mormon council; his manner, however, contradicted his promise, and I have not a doubt he will present himself and induce as many Navajos as he can to be present also. Every prominent man among the Navajos has heard of this Mormon council and doubtless will attend it.

Major Shepherd's column returned to the post yesterday—his report will be forwarded as early as possible.

I am, Very respectfully,
Your Obedient Servant

J. S. SIMONSON
Major, R. M. R.
Commanding troops in the
Navajo County

Lieut. J. D. Wilkins
A. A. Adjutant General,
Dept. of New Mexico

Cañon de Chelly

—Courtesy Southwest Museum.

TO NAVAJO MOUNTAIN

TO NAVAJO MOUNTAIN

Fort Defiance, N. M.
September 20, 1859

Sɪʀ:

In compliance with Orders No. 14, dated Head Quarters Navajo Command, Fort Defiance, N.M., Sept. 1st,
1859, I marched from this camp on the 5th inst. with
Company K, and a detachment of Company E, Mounted
Rifles, and companies C and E, 3rd Infantry, respectively.

The first two days' march (30 miles) and a part of
the third was over the well known Moqui road, but 7
miles beyond the Rio Pueblitas we changed our course
to N. 70° W. and travelling ten miles over a broad valley-
like plain lying between the hills on the Pueblitas on the
east and the range of broken mountain-like hills known
as the *Mesa de la Vaca*[43] on the west, and encamped on

---

[43]Mesas de las Vacas or Black Mesa, is an extended high mesa located in
central-western Navajo country. The late Richard Van Valkenburgh described
this region "as a broad, hand-shaped mesa, across whose 'wrist' runs a pine-
covered rim of generally 8,000 foot elevation. Along its 'fingers' extending to
the southwest lie the Hopi villages and the headwaters of the Polacca, Wepo,

good grass with rain water in holes. Day's march 17 miles.

SEPTEMBER 8.—Marched 11 miles N. 20° W. to the foot of *Mesa de la Vaca,* the northeastern termination, which we supposed to be about 12 miles from the mouth of Cañon de Chelly. Entering this system of broken hills and small valleys, our progress rendered slow by the miry character of the latter from recent heavy rains, we marched on the same course (about N. 20° W.) 10 miles and encamped at a peculiar rock in the valley called *Piedra Santada.*[44] About 5 miles to the north of our camp our Navajo guide says there is a large spring which the Indians call by a name signifying "Trout Spring,"[45] from this fish being found there in abundance. As it lay off our route we did not visit it. We found water in holes at the foot of the rock, but I do not think it permanent. Grass indifferent. Day's march 21 miles.

SEPTEMBER 9.—Travelled 5 miles over the broken mesa. Course N. W., then rising a very steep hill, gradually descended into a broad valley[46] running from N. to S. and extending, as our guide informed us, as far as the Moqui villages. Since entering the *Mesa* we have seen no signs of cultivation except one small patch of corn this morning

Oraibi and Blue Cañon drainages. It is probably the greatest watershed, both in size and capacity in the entire Navajo country." "Notes on the Navajo Country," Richard Van Valkenburgh Collection at the *Arizona Pioneers' Historical Society,* Tucson, Arizona.

[44]Piedra Santada is probably present-day Theater Rock.

[45]Trout Springs is still known by that name, and is designated as such on the Herbert Gregory map of the Navajo country.

[46]First Mesa Wash.

near our camp of last night. This valley, although fertile, is not cultivated, there being no water except in the rainy season, although we found an abundance of rain water in pools along the valley. About 2 miles from where we entered the valley traveling N. 10° W., the guide pointed to a spring of permanent water to the east of our route and about a mile and a half from it, in a cañon at the foot of a high bluff, to which a well beaten trail leads. Marching 8 miles up the valley we encamped on good grass. Water in holes, not permanent. Day's march 13 miles.

SEPTEMBER 10.—Course from camp was N.W. 3 miles up the valley, across a divide and entered another small valley running nearly west, down which we travelled 10 miles, the valley widening as we advanced, until we reached a ruined pueblo of some former race, known now as the pueblo of Iapolate, perched on a hill jutting into the valley on the north side. Nearby is a laguna of permanent water. About a mile above this ruin we left the valley of Iapolate and turning more to the northwest (N. 30° W.) we crossed a "divide" and entered another valley,[47] a tributary of that just left, which the guides informed us debouches on the plain in the neighborhood of *Oraybe,* the most northern of the Moqui villages. Travelling up this vallley (N. 75° W.) 4 miles we encamped on good grass—water in holes, not permanent. Day's march 16 miles.

---

[47]Oraibi Wash,

Three miles from our camp of last night observed bituminous coal of good quality apparently cropping out on the hill side, in two distinct strata, with forty or fifty feet of sandstone intervening.

SEPTEMBER 11.—Travelled 4 miles west, then crossed a divide and entered another small valley, down which we marched three miles, then entered a broken valley running southwest, down which we marched one mile, then turned nearly due west for a short distance, then north west for 7 miles and encamped on good grass—rain water in arroyo. Day's march 17 miles. Saw bituminous coal cropping out along the arroyos at several places today.

SEPTEMBER 12.—Course for 7 miles after leaving camp nearly N.W. to a place with running permanent water, called *Maton de Jara.* Here we observed a column of smoke apparently about 2 miles S.W. which we supposed to be from an Indian camp or signal fire, but after reconnoitering from the top of a neighboring hill our Navajo guide assured us it came out of the earth. This we found to our surprise to be true. That it was a burning coal bed was very evident from the bituminous smell of the smoke which issued from two considerable fissures, the sides of which were coated with the bituminous deposit of the smoke. The hills from the top of which these volumes of smoke issued is forty or fifty feet above the valley, and overgrown with cedar and piñon trees which have been killed by the internal heat. This fire has probably existed for some years as the hill has a considerable cavity on the top from the consumption of the coal which formed the support of a stratum of sandstone and earth. Our guide has not passed this place he says for fifteen years, but at that time there was no such fire, although he has frequently seen similar ones in different places through this country, which he says everywhere abounds in coal, or black earth, as he calls it.

Leaving the burning coal bed we continued our march N. W. 4½ miles to the summit of the principal mountain of the *Mesa de la Vaca* and reaching a plateau on the summit travelled 2½ miles where we reached the bank of a precipice some six or seven hundred feet in height, from which we obtained a view of a vast range of as desolate and repulsive looking country as can be imagined. As far as the eye can reach toward the southwest, west and northwest is a vast mass of sandstone hills without any covering of vegetation except a scanty growth of cedar. In the northwest and apparently about fifty miles distant, *Sierra Panoche*,[48] a detached mountain, looms up, and beyond this and to the northwest, our guide pointed to the junction of Colorado Chiquito and Rio San Juan. At the foot of the precipice lies a valley from a mile to a mile and a half broad which can be traced thirty or

---

[48]Sierra Panoche is none other than Navajo Mountain. Located just north of the Arizona-Utah line and some ninety miles north of Tuba City, this predominating landmark rises to an elevation of 10,416 feet.

This high, rounded, igneous mountain is regarded as sacred by the Navajos. According to Van Valkenburgh, these Indians relate in their Blessing Side stories "that Navajo Mountain represents the head of the female and pollen figure of Navajoland, of which Black Mountain is the body and Malukai Mesa the lower extremities. In ceremonial parlance, the whole system is called *Thadidindzih*, Pollen Mountain." "Notes," Van Valkenburgh Collection, *Arizona Pioneers' Historical Society.*

forty miles to the south where it debouches upon the plains in the neighborhood of the Colorado Chiquito.

Descending the precipice by a steep zig-zag path we reached the valley,[49] and crossing it obliquely to the western side. Two miles from where we entered it, we reached an ancient ruin, like all others in this country, situated on a hill. The buildings are of stone and of the same form and appearance as those met with in the Cañon of Chelly and other parts of New Mexico. Near this ruin we found pure rain water in natural tanks in the sandstone hills, which are solid blocks of unstratified sandstone, which the action of water and other causes have disintegrated into deep fissures and cañons which everywhere break the surface and renders it entirely impracticable to travel over for any distance. Only the bottoms of these cañons can be followed, and the guide assures me that there are very few of them that have any outlet but the mouth. The country on the two sides of this narrow valley have entirely different characteristics. On the eastern side the bluffs of the *Mesa de la Vaca* are of white stratified sandstone, while on the western side the country is a vast mass of red sandstone in the wildest stratal confusion. Camped at the ruined pueblo—day's march 19 miles.

SEPTEMBER 12.—Marched this morning with 20° E. down valley 4 miles to the mouth of a cañon entering from the west which is known by the name of *La Puerta*

---

[49]This is present-day Klethlana Valley, southwest of Kayenta. It separates the rugged northern escarpment of Black Mesa from the extremely dissected country south of Navajo Mountain.

Limita.[50] In this cañon which is of considerable length there is said to be several lagunas and good grazing and is the home of a band of Pah-Utahs. Half mile below the mouth of this cañon is a spring breaking out at the foot of the bluffs on the west side of the valley. Four miles down the valley from the Puerta Limitas, at the point of the mountain, on the west side of the valley, is a laguna of permanent water. From this laguna we changed our course northeast and emerged upon the plain like valley with the *Sana Negra,* a dark rock resembling a vast gothic cathedral, lying due north about ten miles distant. (This rock can be seen eighty or ninety miles from this post.)

Marching six miles N.E. we came to running, and I believe permanent water, near some red hills where we camped on poor grass. Day's march 14 miles.

SEPTEMBER 14.—Course today has been nearly due east along the northern base of the *Mesa de la Vaca* which terminates towards the north in perpendicular precipices from four to seven hundred feet in height. Camped at rain water in holes—grass tolerable. Day's march 18 miles.

SEPTEMBER 15.—One mile and half from camp a laguna of permanent water. About a mile S.S.E. of this laguna the guide pointed to a gorge in the mountain where he says there is a spring called *Ojo Limita.* (Limita is a small red berry intensely acid and valuable as an antiscor-

---

[50]La Puerta Limita is present-day Marsh Pass, running from Klethlana Valley northeast between the red sandstone Segi country and the northern rim of Black Mesa.

butic.) Our road leads S.E. along the base of the bluff of *Mesa de la Vaca,* passing over spurs of slight elevation. Fifteen miles from camp we turned off to a laguna of permanent water, five miles due east where we encamped—grass poor—Day's march 20 miles.

SEPTEMBER 16.—Marched S.E. 9 miles over a broken country to a permanent spring near a solitary rock in the valley, with [an] opening through it like a window. Three miles further came in sight of the cottonwood tree in the Arroyo de Chelly and about 7 miles further we crossed it and encamped on very scanty grass. Day's march 19 miles.

SEPTEMBER 17.—Marched up Arroyo de Chelly, passing numerous corn fields and Navajo huts, swarming with men, women and children whose principal occupation seems to be the devouring of the corn crop of this year. Some of the more provident were engaged in drying corn for winter use in kilns heated with hot stones. The Indians brought us some very good peaches. Half of the Navajo nation seem to be congregated here either to enjoy the fruits of their own labor or the labor of others. They all express good will towards us and a desire to be on friendly terms. Saw a good many horses and two or three flocks of sheep. Marched six miles to the mouth of the cañon and encamped on abundance of coarse bottom grass.

SEPTEMBER 18.—Travelled E. 20° S. for 5 or 6 miles along southern brink of Cañon de Chelly, and every now and then, obtaining a glimpse into the depths of the chasm. About 10 miles from the mouth we passed the point at which Col. Miles' column entered the Cañon last year. About 14 miles from the mouth of the Cañon we found water in the arroyo, perhaps permanent, and at this point we turned to the right, leaving the road by which Col. Miles came from Fort Defiance at the time he entered the Cañon. The road followed by us is the principal one used by the Navajos going from the head to the mouth of the Cañon of Chelly. About 16 miles from our camp of last night we came to the edge of the vast pine forest that extends in a belt of twenty-five miles in breadth from east to west, and in length some eighty miles from north to south. The country to the west of the point first mentioned on the Chelly and Rio Pueblitos provides only cedar and piñon.

About twenty miles from the mouth of the Chelly we came to the head of one of its side cañons, heretofore unknown. It is in some respect more remarkable than the Chelly itself. The road passes within a few yards of its head, a circular opening in the earth fifty or sixty yards in diameter and probably four hundred feet deep. A few hundred yards lower down, the cañon becomes so much contracted and the opposite walls approach each other so nearly that it looks as if one could almost leap across. The falling of even a small stone to the bottom of this curious chasm gives out a report like that of a six pounder. From a hill east of the head of this cañon we could trace its course to its junction with the Cañon de Chelly, about 10 miles to the northwest. Three miles further on we came to a branch of this cañon along which we travelled one or two miles to its head where we encamped. No grass—rain water in the arroyo—permanent water half a mile lower down in the cañoncito, just mentioned. This country has been much grazed over this year and from the great number of hills everywhere seen, must have been a hiding place during the war. The nooks and angles between the Cañon de Chelly and the two side cañons, mentioned above, are doubtless numberless, and being thoroughly known to the Indians and not at all to us, we would have but little chance to ferret them out in time of war. Day's march 25 miles.

SEPTEMBER 19.—Marched S.E. 10 miles to Ewell's Hay Camp[51] and thence to this camp 9 miles. Day's march 19 miles.

Before concluding I would mention that I found no place known to my guides as the "Mesa de Calabaza" mentioned in my instructions and no mountain "supposed to be southwest" where the Navajos are in the habit of taking refuge in time of war, except the *Mesas de la Vacas* themselves. The region of country known by this name is of very considerable extent—say from sixty to seventy miles east and west and of like extent from north to south. The country within these limits is not what is usually known as mesas, or table land, on the contrary its surface is extremely irregular, being everywhere diversified with hills, sometimes rising al-

---

[51]Located some ten miles north of Fort Defiance, Ewell's Hay Camp was one of the post's haying grounds. It was named after Lieutenant Richard S. Ewell, later a general in the Confederate Army.

most to the height of mountains, and cut up with arroyos and divided by valleys. The valleys are without timber, but the hills are clothed with cedar and piñon and now and then a clump of pines, but this is rare. Bituminous coal, apparently of a very fine quality, was observed cropping out along almost every perpendicular bank. In fact this whole region seems to abound in vast coal fields.

No part of this region is now inhabited, except the extreme eastern border, although it was evidently inhabited some years ago, as we saw many abandoned Navajo huts. Our guide says the reason is the Navajos are afraid of the Pah-Utahs upon whose country it borders. There never seems to have been any cultivation here, although the valleys appear to be fertile and produce vast quantities of wild potatoes which we found to be excellent. In all this region we saw no running stream and nothing of permanent water except one, although the guide told of three or four known to him in different parts of this region; that the Navajos would avail themselves of the few watering places in time of war with us and conceal themselves in this labyrinth of hills, valleys and arroyos is very certain, as they have assured me they did last year. Discovering their hiding places would be as difficult as it was to discover Seminoles in the hummocks of Florida.

Beyond the *Mesas de las Vacas* there are one or two cañons mentioned by my guide as having water and grass, but they are within the Pah-Utah country with whom the Navajos have been at war for sometime past.

The command was during its absence without serious sickness and the animals returned in good condition.

The names of places mentioned in this report are the original Indian names translated into Spanish, the Navajo names being frequently harsh and unpronounceable.

Accompanying this is a topographical sketch by Lieutenant Bell, 3rd Infantry, of the country visited by my command and described in the foregoing report.

I am sir,
Very respectfully,
Your ob. servt.
J. G. WALKER
Capt. R. M. R.

SUPPLEMENTARY LETTER

Fort Defiance, N. M.
September 20, 1859

SIR:

On my late exploring expedition in the neighborhood of the Colorado Chiquito and San Juan rivers, my camp was visited about eighty miles west of the mouth of the Cañon de Chelly by a party of Pah Utahs, one of whom could speak the Navajo language, and gave the following statement to my Navajo guide in presence of the interpreter.

That the Mormons had deputed them and some others who had gone on to the Cañon de Chelly, to meet the Navajos and to make peace with them—that they (the Mormons) were anxious to see peace established between all the different tribes between the Colorado and Rio Grande, and by that means to resist the encroachments of the people and government of the United States, the natural enemies of the whole Indian race— that unless they resisted us that we would soon have their entire country—that they (the Mormons) would

assist them with arms and ammunition to do this—That
in order to carry these views fully into effect, the Mormons have sent them (the Pah Utahs) to invite the Navajos to meet them and all the different bands of the
Utahs and Mohaves at the Sierra Panoche, a mountain
some seventy or eighty miles east of the Colorado and
about forty miles southeast of the junction of the Rio San
Juan and Colorado Chiquito. This council is to be held
about the middle of October next, at which time the
Mormons are to distribute arms and ammunition to the
various tribes represented in the council who will join
the alliance.

That this statement is substantially true I have every
reason to believe, as the Pah Utahs to confirm their story,
exhibited various presents from the Mormons such as
new shirts, beads, powder, etc. I have further confirmed
in this opinion by meeting the next day, a deputation of
Navajos on their way to Sierra Panoche to learn the
truth of these statements, which had been conveyed to
them by a Pah Utah Indian whom I saw in the Cañon of
Chelly afterwards, who had been sent as a special envoy
from the Mormons to the Navajos. He had in his pos-
session a letter from a Mormon bishop or elder, stating
that the bearer was an exemplary and regularly baptized member of the Church of Latter Day Saints.

From this there seems little doubt that these fanatics
are endeavoring to combine all the wild tribes of this
region against the people and government of the United
States, and it is to be found that their intrigues will cause
much trouble, unless the government takes prompt and

effective measures to counteract them. It has already been observed that the Navajos since the Mormon emissaries came among them are growing discontented and sullen, and should a war break out between our troops and the tribes I believe it will have been brought about in no inconsiderable degree by Mormon influence and intrigue.[52]

I am, Sir,
Your obt. Servt., etc.
J. G. WALKER
Capt. R.M.R.
Comdg. 2nd. Col. N. C.

Lt. J. H. Edson
Regt. Mtd. Riflemen
Adjt. Navajo Comd.
Fort Defiance, N. M.

---

[52]Reports of Mormon activity among the Navajos was nothing new to the military in New Mexico. As early as March 1856, Indian Agent Henry Linn Dodge claimed to have talked with Indians who had attended Mormon councils. These Navajos stated that missionaries had been very interested about "the Americans that had a fort in Navajo country." Allegedly, the Mormons had asked the Navajos why they did not drive the American soldiers out of their country, for if they permitted them to stay it would not be long before the Navajos lost all their lands.

Both Dodge and Major Kendrick, commanding Fort Defiance, reported seeing during 1856, "a few fine rifles, silver mounted, tobacco, blankets, among the Navajos near Moqui," all allegedly traded from Mormon missionaries from Utah. In January 1858, General John Garland informed the Adjutant General of the Army, "that there was every reason to believe that Brigham Young and his missionaries were stirring up trouble in Navajo country." Garland felt that Latter Day Saints were trying to bring about a peaceful settlement between the Utes and Navajos in an attempt to turn both tribes against the United States government. See Report of Secretary of War, 35th Congress, 2nd Session, *House Executive Document,* Vol. II, pt. II, p. 282.

Mount San Mateo

—Courtesy Southwest Museum.

TO MOUNT SAN MATEO

TO MOUNT SAN MATEO

Fort Defiance, New Mex.
September 25, 1859

SIR:

I have the honor respectfully to report the following in compliance with Orders 14, Head Quarters, Navajo Command, Fort Defiance, N. M. September 1, 1859.

With the command composed of companies B and K, and detachment Company F, 3rd Infantry, officered by Capt. Sykes, Lieut. Freedley and Dickinson, 3rd Infantry and Company H and detachment Company G, Regiment Mounted Riflemen, officered by Lieut. Edson and Claflin of the same Regiment, made the following marches.

SEPTEMBER 5.—Marched from post to Chuska valley. This day's march has nothing worthy of notice, and besides had been frequently passed over by different com-

---

[53]Chuska Valley is shown on a sketch map drawn by Lt. A. W. Whipple in 1855, as lying along the eastern flanks of the Chuska Mountains. It is the area which today extends from Sheep Springs southward to Manuelito Springs. At the time of Shepherd's exploration, the valley was a prime agricultural and grazing locality for the Navajos.

mands last year and this. Direction E.N.E. and distance 14 miles.

SEPTEMBER 6.—Marched eastward first across valley of Chuska, in which were seen several corn fields, not to exceed a hundred acres. Several lodges were seen here, and some apparently friendly Indians were occupying them, it being green corn time. Thence our course passed over the northern slopes of the mountainous mesa, bounding the north of the Bear Springs valley,[54] through which passes the wagon road hence to Albuquerque. The country to the north of our route, was a depressed and rolling plain, extending far in that direction. Encamped in cañon where the water, was said, by the guide Blas Lucero, to be permanent. Direction about east and distance 18 miles. Grass and wood not very abundant.

SEPTEMBER 7.—Marched east and passed over some spurs of the mesa on our right and encamped two mile short of the *Puerto de Aquacito*. The region to the north of our route became more level and appeared like an immense desert, dividing the Navajos from the settlement east of the Sierra de San Mateo.[55] Near our camp were

---

[54]Shepherd has crossed the northern slopes of the Zuñi Mountains. Bear Springs, or Ojo del Oso, was a favorite rendezvous and sacred spot of the Navajos in pre-Anglo days. At that point, Colonel Alexander Doniphan, Narbona, Zarcillas Largas and other Navajo headmen signed a treaty in 1846. With the establishment of Fort Defiance in September 1851, Ojo del Oso became a stopping place on the military road from that post to Albuquerque.

[55]Today known as Mt. Taylor, Mt. San Mateo is a high mountain peak rising 11,389 feet, midway between Albuquerque and Gallup, New Mexico. This barren and deep red peak is regarded by the Navajos as one of their sacred mountains marking the southern boundary of their old country.

corn fields. Direction about east and distance 20 miles. Grass and fuel abundant, water in pool.

SEPTEMBER 8.—Marched E.S.E. In passing through *Puerto de Aquacito* found water, which the guide, Blas, said was permanent. A bed of fine bituminous coal ten feet in thickness cropped out in the ravine, near the spring. About two miles east of this spring was found an old abandoned pueblo, not large, however, nor very old. The land in its vicinity was dry although a corn field a short distance from it was visible. After marching 15 miles we passed over a high ridge, and at 3 miles further on we encamped at rain water pools. Grass and wood good. Direction about E.S.E. and distance 18 miles. Saw today along the route a flock of about 1000 sheep.

SEPTEMBER 9.—Marched 12 miles E.S.E. over high and rolling hills, northern spurs of the mountains to our right. Thence took direction S.E. through two cañons, the latter of which debouched at the northern base of the San Mateo. Encamped at rain water pools. Wood and grass good. The Rio de San Mateo[56] was about a mile in advance, on which there was no wood. Corn field with large and beautiful cieniguillas (meadows) and large corrals and lodges were seen on this river. The old abandoned pueblo was also here found. About a dozen Navajo Indians visited our camp here. They were a portion of Sandoval's band,[57] and were encamped in the latter of

---

[56]Probably the Rio Gallo.
[57]Antonio Sandoval and his band, which has been variously estimated at from 50 to 400 members, were known as *Diné'ana'ih* or Enemy Navajos. This group and its leader were held in contempt by the greater portion of the tribe because of

the two cañons passed through. At a point between the two cañons, I took Lieut. Claflin with ten mounted men and diverged to the left of our trail and visited the Rita de San Lucas, expecting to find Indians and corn fields, but saw neither. A heavy trail passed thence over the Sierra de San Mateo to the town of Cebolleta.[58] Direction today nearly East and distance 23 miles. Some mules gave out today, although but half laden.

The whole route thus far had the most numerous and heavily beaten trails I have ever seen in the Navajo country, and it is evidently the great thoroughfare for all thefts and robberies.

SEPTEMBER 10.—Marched south across the valley and ascended the western slope of San Mateo. Ascent about two thousand feet with footway good and much travelled over by Indians. This trail led to the valley of Cuvero,[59] and Laguna.[60] After about three miles from first

---

their repeated alliances with the Spanish, Mexicans, and later, the Anglo-Americans. Sandoval and his band continually raided their brethren in Navajo-land for slaves and livestock, which were sold in the Mexican settlements along the Rio Grande Valley.

[58]Cebolleta is located on the east slopes of the Cebolleta Mountains, thirteen miles north of Laguna Pueblo. Around 1744 a Franciscan Mission was established there for the Navajos but was soon discontinued because of Navajo disinterest. Thereafter, the community became a frontier outpost for Spanish military operations against the Navajos. With commencement of the Mexican Period in 1821, this town became a favorite resort of traders and procurers of Indian slaves, and continued as such well into the Anglo-American Period.

[59]Cubero or Cuvero, was founded in the 18th Century, and was named for the Spanish Governor, Don José Cubero. Because of its proximity to the Navajos, this town was frequently raided. In his *Memoir of a Tour of Northern Mexico in 1846-47*, A. Wislizenus wrote: "This [Cubero] being a frontier settlement, the people have greatly suffered from the incursions of the Navajos; occasionally they have been driven from their village to take refuge in the cliffs. The Navajos

ascent, the trail led down, by a rough and rocky foot way, to a deep gorge of the mountain, in which was a small *cieniguilla* and some pasturage. Many lodges were seen scattered through the forest, and were used probably as a summer resort. Thence ascended by the trail, the mountain again, and at about ten miles at the southern edge of it, we descended to the Rio Gallo by a rough and unfrequented route. Direction today about S.S.W. and distance 25 miles. Day's journey very fatiguing to men and pack animals.

SEPTEMBER 11.—Laid by today on account of rain and the fatigue of the animals and men. Procured from Cuvero another guide, Fernando Aragon.[61]

SEPTEMBER 12.—Marched twelve miles between fields of lava and the Sierra de Acoma. Trail good and easy. Encamped at rain water pool. Grass indifferent, fuel abundant. A large ranchería of corrals and lodges was at this camp. Direction south.

SEPTEMBER 13.—Marched for about ten miles; when we reached the valley of *Cebolla Chiquita*, where were found a large and beautiful *cieniguilla* and some corrals and lodges, the latter mostly new or of last winter's make,

are not always hostile. They frequently visited the village on friendly terms, and probably, the inhabitants by trade with them, have made as much peace as war"
[60]The Pueblo of Laguna is located on the Rio San José, fifty miles west of Albuquerque; and was established about 1697 by Keres Indians fleeing from the Spanish re-conquest of New Mexico.
[61]A noted Indian trader, Fernando Aragon, was often utilized as a guide and tracker by the U.S. Army during its early-day operations against the Navajos. When not employed by the government, however, Aragon often organized volunteer expeditions against the Navajos to procure slaves and livestock, which he profitably bartered to New Mexican ranchers and householders.

showing that a number of Navajos had wintered there during the last war with them.

The guide Aragon said the same. After passing this valley we crossed a western spur of the mountains and descended into the mouth of the valley of the Cebolla Grande. Encamped at rain water pond at point of Lava. Wood and grass good. direction S. S. West and distance 18 miles.

SEPTEMBER 14.—Marched along the *"Mal Paiz,"*[62] or field of lava for six miles, when the trail led across a broad plain. Encamped at some rain water ponds at the edge of the timber on the ridge seperating the waters of the Pacific from those of the Atlantic. Route mostly level. Direction about S.W. and distance 24 miles. Wood and grass good. Shortly after leaving camp the fresh tracks of three mounted Indian ponies were seen. On starting from camp in the morning I took Lieut. Claflin and ten mounted men, and went up the valley of the Cebolla Grande to the head spring, and found that no Navajos had fled there during the war last winter. Distance up to the spring about eight miles out of the line of march.

SEPTEMBER 15.—Marched on old trail from Acoma[63] to the Rita Quemado. Direction about S.W. and en-

[62]The extensive field of lava or *Mal Paiz* (bad lands), is located about ten miles south of Mt. Taylor. This lava field is represented with this brief notation on the map prepared by Topographical Engineer, James H. Simpson: "Lava formation of an interesting character."

[63]This Keres pueblo is situated on a rocky mesa, 357 feet in height, about sixty miles west of the Rio Grande, in Valencia County, New Mexico. Its strong defensive position and inaccessibility has given this pueblo the ability to withstand all encroachments by other Indian tribes, as well as the Spanish and Anglo-Americans.

camped down stream about a mile. Distance 19 miles.
Wood and grass good. Found no Indians had been living
here, contrary to what was supposed, probably being too
near the Apaches. It is perhaps a neutral ground judging
from the abundance of Antelope there.

SEPTEMBER 16.—Marched down Valley of Rita Quemado, and found that its waters sunk or spread out in a
small lake at five miles, instead of running for thirty miles
as was supposed. Encamped at some rain water ponds.
Wood and grass good. Direction W.N. West and distance 18 miles.

SEPTEMBER 17.—Marched for four miles west, when we
reached the Saline Lake,[64] having an old crater, one hundred and fifty feet high in the center of which there is
a pond of very hot saline water at the bottom. This pool
is about 200 feet long by 150 feet broad and from ten to
fifteen feet deep. The surface appears to be at a higher
elevation than the water of the surrounding lake, which
has a circumference of about ten miles. All these waters
hold so much salt in solution as to prevent a person from
sinking below the surface. At this season of the year
there is so large a supply of rain water in the great lake,
as to have dissolved a greater portion of the crystaliza-
tion, and what remains lies embedded within the soft
mud covering the bottom of the lake, to what depth is
not known. The salt crystals are easily gathered by scrap-
ing them out of the mud with the hands. The guide Ar-

---

[64]This salt deposit had long been utilized by both Spanish and Indian alike.
In mid-July 1855 Navajos were prohibited its use by the Meriwether Treaty,
which clearly defined that tribe's eastern boundaries. Governor David Meriwether, however, granted Navajos permission to gather salt there, as it would not

gon gathered a small sack full in this manner, it was found white and pure and very palatable. At any season of the year the salt can thus be gathered.

The water within the crater has no crystallization though exceedingly saline. As it is a large spring, its waters probably percolates through the scoria, which forms the crater into the large outer lake. This main outer lake appears itself to be the bed of a large crater, having its surrounding sides of volcanic rock. There is no permanent water flowing from the exterior into the larger lake. A small fresh water spring exists among the rocks on the southwestern side of the outer crater, but its waters never reach the lake. This spring was amply sufficient for the uses of the command.

The vicinity of the lake may be distinguished by a high mesa lying about three miles south of the lake, with a conical peak of the same height, situated between it and the lake. Heavy trails lead from the salina to the south and to the west towards the Rio Colorado Chiquito about two days journey west; and east towards Cuvero, and north towards Zuñi—all showing it to be much frequented.

SEPTEMBER 18.—Marched from salina and took the heavy and well beaten trail in the direction of the Pueblo of Zuñi. After crossing for ten miles a broad valley formed by the junction of the valley of the Rita Quemado and

interfere with any vested right, because the lake was not within the land grant claimed by Zuñi; and under the laws of Spain and Mexico, all salt deposits were considered "common property." See: David Meriwether to George Manypenny, July 27, 1855; *National Archives,* Records of Office of Indian Affairs, Record Group 75, New Mexico Superintendency Papers, Letters Received.

one running from the east, we ascended a high mesa and thence descended into a parallel valley, on the northern side of which we found permanent water running from a cañon. At the mouth of this cañon and situated on top of the mesa, are the ruins of an old abandoned pueblo. From the remains of the walls still standing it must have been beautifully built of volcanic rock of which the mesa is underlaid. During the occupancy of the pueblo, the broad valley below was probably cultivated. It is now too dry for such purposes. Wood, water and grass good. Direction about N. N. West and distance 22 miles.

Near this camp but west of it, the late Capt. Dodge, Navajo Indian Agent, was killed by Apaches in November 1856, while enroute to visit the salina, in company with Major Kendrick,[65] U.S.A., then commanding this post.

SEPTEMBER 19.—Continued march upon Zuñi trail and after passing two lofty mountains (mesas), reached Zuñi. Direction north and distance 23 miles.

SEPTEMBER 20-22.—Was occupied in marching from Zuñi to this post, a distance of 60 miles over the wagon road, the trails being impracticable for want of water for so large a command. This part of the route is too well known to require further notice. Total distance marched 317 miles.

Judging from the absence of signs on the route from the Acoma Mountains to the Pueblo of Zuñi, the Nava-

[65]Henry Linn Kendrick, of New Hampshire, graduated from West Point in July 1835, and was assigned to the Second Infantry. A year later he was transferred to the Second Artillery; and remained with that regiment throughout the

joes do not frequent the region south of the Zuñi Mountains, although the climate is warm and the pasturage abundant during the winter months.

Very Respectfully
Your obt. Servt. etc.

O. L. SHEPHERD
Capt. 3rd Inf. & Bvt. Maj.
Comdg. 1st. Col. Expl. Expedition.

Lt. J. H. Edson
Regt. Mtd. Riflemen
Adjt., Navajo Comd.

Mexican War. Kendrick began his duty in New Mexico in 1849; and was with Colonel John M. Washington's expedition into Navajoland. Two years later he participated in Colonel Edwin Sumner's campaign against the tribe; and assumed command of newly established Fort Defiance a year later. Kendrick remained at that isolated post until 1857, at which time he was granted a professorship of chemistry at West Point. For additional details see: Marvin Vincent and Samuel Tillman, *Col. Henry L. Kendrick, U.S.A.* (New York: Dutton, 1892).

INDEX

INDEX

BOOKS OF THE WEST . . . FROM THE WEST

CONNECTICUT COLLEGE LIBRARY   dc
917.91 W152
The Navajo reconnaissance;

3 1839 001628662

DATE DUE

MR 13'68			
JUN 0 1 2001			
GAYLORD			PRINTED IN U.S.A.

917.91
W152   245933

917.91		245933
W152		
AUTHOR		
Walker		ʼ ₁
TITLE		
The Navajo reconnaissance		
DATE DUE	**BORROWER'S NAME**	
MR 12 '68	WORK ROOM	
	NEW BOOK	
MR 13 '68		

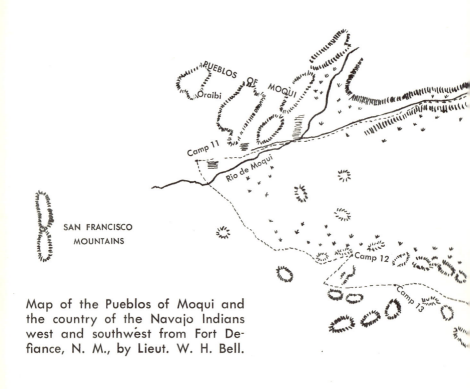

PUEBLOS OF MOQUI
Oraibi
Camp 11
Rio de Moqui
SAN FRANCISCO MOUNTAINS
Camp 12
Camp 13

Map of the Pueblos of Moqui and the country of the Navajo Indians west and southwest from Fort Defiance, N. M., by Lieut. W. H. Bell.